LP

C000194216

Eric Heffer has been Labour MP for the Walton Division of Liverpool since 1964. He worked as a joiner until 1964 and was a Liverpool City Councillor between 1960 and 1966. He was Labour front bench spokesman on Industrial Relations between 1970 and 1972 and served as a Minister of State under Tony Benn in the Department of Industry between 1974 and 1975. For the past eleven years he has served on the NEC of the Labour Party and was Chair of the Party in 1983-4. He has written widely for various newspapers and magazines and is the author of *The Class Struggle in Parliament* (Victor Gollancz, 1973).

Acknowledgements

I would like to thank all those who have contributed in various ways towards making this book possible. My thanks are due especially to the Library Staff of the House of Commons who have untiringly assisted me to find the books, newspaper articles and reports I needed. I wish to thank also those who have unhesitatingly agreed to allow me to quote from their articles and books. My thanks are also due to Colin Robinson, my editor, who after reading the manuscript suggested some cuts which were essential to bring the numbers of words down to a more manageable level. In particular, I wish to thank my wife Doris who typed and re-typed the book, working long hours under great duress due to the time factor involved. Thanks must also go to Janet Burgess who towards the final type stage willingly came in and re-typed several chapters. I also wish to thank Robin Blackburn who, after reading the book, made many constructive suggestions to improve it. The content of the book, of course, is entirely my responsibility. If there are any brickbats to be thrown at what it says, then they must be thrown at me. It could be suggested that the book is a rehash of old socialist concepts. I believe they are socialist concepts updated to modern times. One thing is for sure, they are, I trust, socialist, and I am by no means ashamed of that.

Labour's Future
Socialist or SDP Mark 2?

Eric S. Heffer

VERSO
The imprint of New Left Books

First published 1986

© Eric S. Heffer 1986

Verso 15 Greek Street, London W1V 5LF

Typeset in Times by
Leaper & Gard Ltd, Bristol, England

Printed by Thetford Press,
Thetford, Norfolk

ISBN 0 86091 166 7
ISBN 0 86091 878 5 (Paperback)

Contents

Dedication

To all those good comrades, past and present who have fought the good fight to achieve a democratic socialist society. In particular, to those in the City of Liverpool, and especially the 49 Labour Councillors, who have shown great courage and determination in the struggle against the evils of the Tory capitalist system.

Introduction

This book is a response to developments in policy and organisation which have taken place in the Labour Party in recent years. The Party has long been a type of political coalition, with strong socialist and non-socialist currents, uneasily existing side by side within it. The socialist current, whilst immensely influential and almost dominant for a short time, has never really had control of the Party, and when it looked as if it might, sections of the right-wing, non-socialist current split away.

What we are witnessing to-day is the transformation of the Party into another SDP, a party which, although retaining a written socialist Constitution, finds it is increasingly being ignored. The difference between past and present periods of revisionism is that those who carried out the revisionist policies in the past were strongly combatted, whereas to-day they are virtually unopposed, because everyone in the Party wants to defeat Thatcherism at the next General Election, and no-one wants to be accused of rocking the boat.

What is happening to the Labour Party in Britain, however, is not an isolated event. It has already occurred in practically every socialist or social-democratic Party in Europe. The Labour Party, until recently, was considered to be to the left of most of the socialist Parties in Europe, and certainly to the left of the Euro-Communist Parties. That claim cannot now be sustained. The reasons for this are examined in what follows.

Most of this book was written in early 1986. Since then, a

whole series of developments have taken place, which underline its theme. The NEC has received a majority and minority Report on Liverpool, it has continued with the suspension of the Liverpool City Party and has expelled supporters of the Militant Tendency in Liverpool. Other left-wingers (by no means all Militant supporters) have been expelled or are under threat of expulsion in other parts of the country. An atmosphere of witch-hunting is developing, and is directed against all the so-called 'hard-left'.

The opinion polls, which are now central to Labour's campaigning, seem to be dominating the political thinking of some in the Party leadership, and although the Party appears to be doing better in the polls, the Leader's personal rating remains below that of the Party. Writers like Peter Kellner of the *New Statesman*, strongly argue that the more Militant supporters are expelled, the more support the Party gets. The havoc such expulsions create amongst Party members and activists is totally disregarded.

The press have also suggested that the Shadow Cabinet wants to drop policy commitments, except the reduction of long-term unemployment and the anti-poverty programme. Roy Hattersley underlined this when he spoke in the budget debate on the 19th March 1986, 'If, as I and as my Party believes, the national resources that are available were concentrated, to the exclusion of other objectives, in the reduction of long term unemployment, the anti-poverty programme ...' The truth is, the NEC have not up to the time of writing discussed the issue, and when I tried to raise it at the Finance and General Purposes Committee of the NEC, a majority present voted to exclude any reference to it from the minutes of the meeting. It is, therefore, not only Michael Heseltine who can complain about Cabinet minutes being doctored, a similar charge could be made about those minutes.

In the *Socialist Register 1985/86*,[1] Marcel Liebman in his essay, 'Reformism yesterday and Social Democracy To-day', writes that before 1914, 'All the different currents and tendencies within social democracy agreed that bourgeois society should be undermined from within. The distinction between

---

1. *Socialist Register 1985/86*. Social Democracy and After. Edited by Ralph Milliband, John Savile, Marcel Liebman, Leo Panitch. The Merlin Press 1986

reformist and revolutionary tendencies was less clear than it might now seem. ... For many people the question of reform or revolution was not posed in clear terms, and the changes likely to result from the actions of the socialist movement (and those which had already occured) seemed to guarantee that the world would be completely transformed. Given that seemed certain, the question of means (legal or otherwise, violent or non-violent) lost much of its relevance'.

He argues later that the situation has radically changed. He says that 'The problem of how to use and control the masses was one of the main elements influencing the problematic and dynamic of social democracy.. ... Once it had abandoned the call to the masses and even the threat of making such a call, social democratic tactics were designed to make gains within the neo-capitalist society in which the mixed economy gave the administrators who had emerged from its ranks a relatively important role. This was the positional warfare described by Gramsci. ... without the fighting'. He goes on 'This development meant more than the end of any vision of socialism in the sense that the founders of socialism and the early reformists understood the term'.

Liebman argues that, at best, the present day social democrats (meaning those who still call themselves socialist) hope to hold Parliamentary power for a period, and that their insistence on moderation and their desire for appeasement normally leads them to adopt policies which capitalist rightist governments never seriously dream of rejecting.

The 1945/51 Labour Government did begin a serious transformation of society, and that is why Thatcher is attempting to carry out a counter-revolution, but can we be sure that Labour will contemplate radical change in the future? If one drops all commitments, apart from improving pensions and helping the long term unemployed, then one is operating within the parameters of acceptance of the capitalist system, with no fundamental transformation of society in mind. Marcel Liebman is unfortunately proved right.

The French Socialist Government proved a great disappointment. Its recent defeat undoubtedly resulted from its failure to maintain its early Socialist policies and its retreat into an acceptance of bourgeois economic policies.

Without any discussions of any kind with them, I find that Marcel Liebman and John Saville, in the final essay in the

current *Socialist Register,* argue for 'revolutionary reformism', a concept I advanced some years back, and with which I end this book. They say, 'It should be said that 'revolutionary reformism' does not postulate a smooth and uneventful transition to socialism by way of electoral support and parliamentary majorities ...
... 'revolutionary reformism' is also bound to be very conscious of the fact that any serious challenge to dominant classes must inevitably create resistance and will be determined to meet that resistance with every weapon that it requires, including of course the mobilisation of mass support'. It is good to see that the crisis in the socialist movement is meeting similar responses from other socialists.

Since writing this book, the question of what will happen in Britain after the next General Election has come to the fore increasingly. A future coalition government is being mooted from differing political positions, including by Anthony Barnett whose view on this I find confused and unacceptable (see chapter 13). It is possible that no single party will have an overall majority in the House of Commons after the next election, but that cannot be said with any certainty and I believe it is wrong for much to be made of it, certainly not by anyone claiming to be a left-wing socialist. The real danger of a coalition is surely from the SDP/Liberal alliance. David Steel, on a television programme recently, said that unofficial and informal contacts and discussions were being held between senior politicians of all parties. Who in the Labour Party, one wonders, is talking to Centre Forward Tories and Alliance politicians? Labour must surely reject such ideas, and that is all the more reason why socialist objectives must be essential to Labour's policies. If they are not, then objections to coalition cannot really be sustained.

In the pamphlet *A Million Jobs a Year*[2] published by the Campaign Group of MPs for consideration by the labour movement, Andrew Glyn states that 'The problem of reaching full employment is fundamentally one of political determination'. That surely means socialist planning, and a development of public ownership. To suggest unemployment can be dealt with in any other way is a sham. Boldness and determination are essential. In 1945, the Labour Government faced immense

---

2. *A Million Jobs a Year — The Case for Full Employment* by Andrew Glynn. Verso 1985.

problems. The Labour Party put forward a Manifesto called *Let us Face the Future*. It was issued on the authority of the NEC, and was discussed and agreed by the Annual Conference of the Labour Party over Whitsun 1945. The NEC asked for it to be considered not only by the labour movement, but by all men and women, at home and in the Services. It was, and it won their support. It was not a mealy-mouthed manifesto. It said, 'The Labour Party is a socialist Party, and proud of it. Its ultimate purpose at home is the establishment of the Socialist Commonwealth of Great Britain — free, democratic, efficient, progressive, public-spirited, its material resources organised in the service of the British people'.

Its policy was bold. It put forward a programme of public ownership. It called for supervision of monopolies and cartels, for a programme for the export trade, for economic and price controls, and for a better organisation of government departments. It developed a policy for agriculture, for housing and a building programme; it pledged the party to work towards land nationalisation, to develop the Education Act, to create a National Health Service and, a Social Security system, and to work for a world of progress and peace. It ended by a call to all progressives for support of the principles of policy set out in the Manifesto.

We cannot turn the clock back, but we can learn both from our successes and failures in the past. If the Labour Government could carry out its commitments in 1945, under great difficulties and with 'moderates' leading the Party, why should we expect less to-day? We should not act like mesmerised rabbits in front of Mrs Thatcher's stoat. We should fight to get rid of the threat, as the Labour Government did with Churchill in 1945. Labour today is at the crossroads. Only boldness and socialist conviction can win it support.

1
Labour's Socialist Objectives

The seeds of socialism are historically deeply rooted amongst the British people. Fenner Brockway's book about the Levellers and Diggers[1] of the English Revolution of 1640 refers to them as the first socialists. The British people and the working class in particular have fought bitter battles to achieve their democratic rights. It is important to recall the Putney Debates in the New Model Army in 1647, when a sharp clash took place between soldiers on the one hand and General Ireton and Oliver Cromwell on the other. The soldiers claimed the right to suffrage for every free born Englishman, a right denied by Cromwell who argued that suffrage must be based on property, not natural right.

Colonel Thomas Rainborough, who was a Commander of a foot regiment, put the soldiers' case: 'I think that the poorest he that is in England has a life to live, as the greatest he; and therefore truly sir, I think it clear, that every man that is to live under a Government ought first by his own consent to put himself into that Government; and I do think that the poorest man in England is not at all bound in a strict sense to that Government that he hath not had a voice to put himself under.'

Socialism is not an alien outside influence, it is a product of the class struggle in Britain. The English Civil War and Revolu-

---

1. *Britain's First Socialists* by Fenner Brockway. Quartet Books 1980.

tion of the seventeenth century set the scene for the growth of
the capitalist system but they also sowed the seeds of a great
socialist tradition.

British socialists and trade unionists together created the
Labour Party. From the very beginning the Party was based on
the organised working-class. The Independent Labour Party,
Social Democratic Federation and Fabians in their own ways
introduced socialist ideas into the Party whilst the unions gave it
a mass base. It would be wrong, however, to believe that the
unions did not make any contribution to socialist ideas. For
example it was the Gas Workers Union, (now the GMBATU)
whose rules contained the statement, 'the interests of all
workers are one. ... a wrong done to any kind of Labour is
wrong done to the whole of the working class... Victory or
defeat of any portion of the Army of Labour is a gain or loss to
the whole of that Army, which by its organisation and union is
marching steadily and irresistibly forward to its ultimate goal —
the Emancipation of the working-class. That Emancipation can
only be brought about by the strenuous and united efforts of the
working class itself. WORKERS UNITE.' It is a tragedy that
these words were not fully accepted by the entire movement
during the miners' strike in 1984/85.

It has often been said that the Labour Party, like the Church of
England, or more strictly, the Anglican Communion, is a Broad
Church. That is true and within its ranks, from the day it was
formed, there have been Marxists, Methodists, Atheists, Roman
Catholics, Moslems, etc. The one thing that has united them has
been the desire to create a socialist society based on Clause IV of
the Constitution.

The Labour Party, especially since 1918, has openly declared
its belief in socialism. The Party Programme of 1982, which is
still Party policy, says: 'The Labour Party is a democratic socialist party and proud of it. Our objective is to create a classless
society, where all may live a full and varied life. Our priority is
to bring about a fundamental and irreversible shift in the
balance of power and wealth in favour of working people and
their families.'

Socialism is enshrined in Clause IV of the Party Constitution.
It contains the Party Objects which are: '(1) To organise and
maintain in Parliament and in the country a Political Labour
Party. (2) To co-operate with the General Council of the Trades
Union Congress, or other kindred organisations, in joint politi-

cal or other action in harmony with the Party Constitution and Standing Orders. (3) To give effect as far as may be practicable to the principles from time to time approved by the Party Conference. (4) To secure for the workers by hand or by brain the full fruits of their industry and the most equitable distribution thereof that may be possible upon the basis of the common ownership of the means of production, distribution and exchange, and the best obtainable system of popular administration and control of each industry or service, and (5) Generally to promote the political, social and economic emancipation of the people, and more particularly of those who depend upon their own exertions by hand or by brain for the means of life.'

Whilst the objects are not Marxist in language, in essence they add up to class politics — politics on behalf of the working-class and their allies. The Labour Party believes in the transformation of society, the ending of the capitalist system, and the creation of a new socialist society, democratic and pluralist, based upon the organised working class. To achieve that new society, Labour believes it should use the ballot box, but in addition, must also involve itself in extra-parliamentary activity such as demonstrations, marches, strikes, petitions, pickets, lobbies and so on. The two are not contradictory, they are complimentary.

The struggle for socialism is long and hard, there are no short cuts. It began only when the capitalist system came into existence. It could not be otherwise. The economic and political conditions necessary to create socialism were not there earlier. They are today, and socialism therefore should clearly be high on the Agenda.

Keir Hardie, a founder of the Labour Party, outlined what Socialism was when he wrote in his little book *From Serfdom to Socialism*,[2] 'To the Socialist the community represents a huge family organisation in which the strong should employ their gifts in promoting the wealth of all, instead of using their strength for their own personal aggrandisement.' He further wrote, 'The economic object of Socialism, therefore, is to make land and industrial capital common property, and to cease to produce for the profit of the landlord and the capitalist and to begin to produce for the use of the community.'

---

2. *From Serfdom to Socialism* by J. Keir Hardie. George Allen (London) 1907.

Since it was formed in 1900, the Labour Party has achieved a great deal, particularly after 1945, when the reformist Attlee Government took office. That Government did not create a classless socialist society, but it took Britain falteringly along that road with the Welfare State, National Health Service, extended public ownership programme, Local Authority housing policies and educational reform. Unfortunately after a few years, when it should have moved further ahead, it hesitated, settling for Herbert Morrison's 'consolidation' and instead of a socialist Britain, it developed a welfare capitalist State, with a small number of socialist oases in its midst. Welfare capitalism existed until the counter-revolution of Mrs Thatcher, when the whole structure was undermined and radically changed.

Socialism is on the agenda today because welfare capitalism can no longer deliver. Government intervention in economic affairs as outlined by Keynes is no longer adequate. The crisis of capitalism, both economic and political, is such that tinkering with the system cannot, even temporarily, solve anything. Only with democratic socialist planning, together with increased political democracy, can we begin to deal with Britain's problems, and even then they cannot be dealt with in isolation.

Despite Labour governments Britain remains a class-ridden society. Democratic socialists believe it is essential to end class society. Socialism cannot be achieved unless that happens and genuine equality of opportunity cannot be created while class divisions exist. Class society arises because the ownership of the means of production, distribution and exchange is in the hands of a relatively small group. The socialist case for public ownership is not based on the need for greater efficiency; efficiency — or inefficiency — can apply either to public or private companies. Public ownership is necessary in order to eliminate class divisions and to end privilege. It is impossible to create a classless society whilst private ownership of major industries exists.

The Labour Party's call for public ownership does not necessarily imply nationalization. There are many forms of public ownership, ranging from the nationalization of an entire industry or groups of companies to municipal or co-operative ownership, or even semi-public ownership, with a minority holding by private interests. It is essential that there should be these varying forms of public ownership if we are to avoid the octopus-like tentacles of bureaucracy. The experiences of the East European communist states show us that whilst it is important to create a society where the state has a positive role to play, the state must not, at the same time, be all-pervading.

The first task, then, in the creation of a socialist society, is the development of public ownership in many and varying forms which eliminate the power and influence of the capitalist class. Secondly, to avoid the creation of a new bureaucratic ruling class, it is necessary to create forms of democratic management. There are a lot of misconceptions about what is meant by industrial democracy and workers' control. Industrial democracy can mean nothing more than an extension of free collective bargaining. It can mean that by right, workers receive more information, participate in establishing planning agreements, and have a greater say in health, safety and welfare matters. It can also mean that workers have representatives on boards of directors. Under workers' control, a workforce can, by the use of industrial muscle, force management to do what they want in relation to certain specific decisions. However, strictly speaking, none of this is democratic or, put differently, self-management. Yet it is self-management which will have to be created if bureaucracy is to be avoided and workers are to participate in real decision-making.

A system of elections for workers' councils is required. These councils will either manage industry themselves or exercise control over managers. There is no need to lay down a blueprint for this. Experiments can be made, some based on the system of workers' councils in Yugoslavia, others more clearly allied to methods of election in our municipal authorities. It is important that such self-management is integrated into a national plan of production if we are to avoid syndicalism where workers are not concerned with society as a whole, but only with their own interests in the factory.

The trade unions will have a vital role to play in any system of self-management. Unlike their Soviet counterparts British trade unions must never become a part of the state machinery. Theirs must be an independent existence and role so that they can provide the necessary checks and balances to the elected government and to worker's councils in factories or industries. Even in a workers' state, workers will require organizations to protect themselves from their own state apparatus. They will have to struggle to ensure that state power and control are slowly reduced until they are almost non-existent and government by the people becomes a reality. The trade unions in a socialist society can and will play an important part in welfare arrangements, in health legislation, in negotiating rates of pay and conditions of employment. But they will also be an important centre of power within the overall democratic structure of society.

The third vital ingredient of democratic socialism is democracy itself. There cannot be socialism without democracy. The two are indivisible. That is why the East European communist governments are wrong when they claim that their societies are socialist because there is public ownership with a planned economy. They are of course fully supported in this claim by most of our media, who are only too keen to equate socialism with the bureaucratic system of the Soviet Union and the other East European states.

The fourth essential for democratic socialism is internationalism, in outlook and action. This involves adopting a long-term strategy for a Socialist Europe, in contrast to the Common Market which fosters and protects capitalism. It also involves campaigning for peace. We should have as an objective a nuclear-free Europe. Detente must be worked for and, ultimately the NATO and Warsaw Pacts dismantled. A beginning to this can be made with a reduction in the armed forces of both East and West: all nuclear weapons and bases should be dismantled from the Russian/Polish borders in the East to the Portuguese coast and Britain in the West. Socialism cannot be created unless peace prevails. To live in harmony with one's international neighbours is a basic socialist objective.

Socialism, therefore, is a society without class divisions, without social hatred and prejudice, without poverty and misery for the many and riches and privilege for the few. It is a society where genuine freedom for the individual is guaranteed as part of the collective freedom for all. Where people accept the concept that they are their brother's and sister's keeper, and where nations live together without threatening each other, and war is a thing of the past.

Again, Keir Hardie put it succinctly, when he wrote 'Socialism implies the inherent equality of human beings. It does not assume that all are alike, but only that all are equal. Holding this to be true of individuals, the Socialist applies it also to races. Only by a full and unqualified recognition of this claim can peace be restored to the world. Socialism implies brotherhood and brotherhood implies a recognition of the fact that the duty of the strong is not to hold the weak in subjection, but to assist them to rise higher and ever higher in the scale of humanity, and this cannot be done by trampling upon and exploiting their weakness but by caring for them and showing them the better way.'

Unfortunately, socialism has not been established in any part of the world. There have been successful social democratic governments, like those in Sweden, which have humanized capitalism without ending it, and there are other governments which have made advances towards creating a socialist society but for various reasons have either been defeated or have retreated, sometimes in shame. Social democracy has not enjoyed great success as the recent French experience has shown. The countries where social democracy has held sway have not been transformed into socialist societies. Neither has socialism been created in Eastern Europe. The countries of the Warsaw Pact may have socialised economies of varying degrees, but societies which have camps for political oppositionists, or where political dissidents are jailed or sent to psychiatric hospitals, and where freedom of expression does not exist, cannot by any stretch of the imagination be considered socialist. Socialism means free institutions, free and independent trade unions, free elections, free expression and freedom to organise. It means the flowering of the human spirit, not its stifling by a bureaucratic state apparatus, based on a one party system.

At the moment, Britain has the highest level of unemployment ever recorded in the nation's history. Riots break out in the inner city areas, the youth in particular are without hope; educational opportunities are stifled; people are living in rotten housing conditions, thousands are homeless; the threat of nuclear war hangs over our heads, racism is on the increase, and the economic crisis deepens.

British capitalism's decline can be traced back to 1870 when Britain stopped being the workshop of the world. In *Britain in Decline*[3], published in 1981, Andrew Gamble writes, 'The failure to maintain superiority in productivity and in manufacturing has caused a steep fall in the importance of the British economy in the world economy and in its share of world trade'. He provides a table which shows the values of world exports by manufactur-

---

3. *Britain in Decline* by Andrew Gamble. The Macmillan Press 1981.

ing nations 1899-1979 in percentages. The UK in 1899 had 33.2%. In 1950 it was 25.5% and in 1979 went down to 9.7%. Germany on the other hand was 7.3% in 1950 and in 1979 had gone up to 20.8%. France had remained almost static in these years, and Japan had gone from 3.4% in 1950 to 13.6% in 1979.

Gamble points out that real take-home pay for the workers has virtually stagnated, whilst unemployment is worse than most other major capitalist economies. He rightly argues that the 'decline cannot be reduced to technical issues and remedies' and cites the Brookings Report on the British economy which rejected technical explanations and concluded that 'Britain's economic malaise stems largely from its productivity problems whose origins lie deep in the social system'.

There is only one answer. Only socialist policies can deal with the crisis. Clearly, the Labour Party in government must go beyond Roosevelt New Dealism. Its first task must be to restore the welfare state, and to take back into public ownership those industries which have been privatised. It must introduce controls on the export of capital abroad, and restore to the trade unions the rights denied them by the Thatcher Government. It must put people back to work by a policy of investment, especially in the labour intensive industries such as construction and housing. It must have a truly socialist perspective for the transformation of capitalism into socialism. This will meet with tremendous resistance, both at home and abroad. The fact that Britain is part of the EEC, with its Community laws, is bound to create problems and we shall also meet great difficulties from the USA.

We should never forget what happened to President Allende and his Popular Unity Government in Chile. Allende was a democratically elected President, but from the day he assumed office there were strong forces, native and foreign, who went out of their way to destabilise his regime. The CIA and the multi-national companies were in active opposition and, eventually, the democratically elected President was overthrown by the Generals.

A Labour Government which is serious about carrying out its programme must prepare the people in advance for the sort of difficulties it will undoubtedly face. To fail to do so can only, in the last analysis, lead to disillusionment. There are, of course, those who say it is impossible for us to carry out a socialist policy because we could never get away with it, that the forces ranged against us are much too powerful. Therefore, they argue, Labour should drop its socialism, or at least say little about it, and then we can win government. Yes, we might win, but we would no longer be a socialist party, we would be a Social Democratic Party Mark 2, and socialist policies and objectives would be cast aside, just as Dr David Owen and Mrs Shirley Williams have cast them aside in the SDP.

Labour must reaffirm its socialist principles, policies and objectives. Apart from anything else, no-one will believe us if we try to disown these principles, whilst our constitution and programme continue to advocate socialism. The Tories attack us for being a party run by trade union leaders, a party which wants to introduce an East European type state, which rejects democracy, and which is totally bureaucratic. Although none of this is true, of course, they will continue saying it, and will be helped by the media and the press. They will also claim that Labour's policies are full-blooded socialist, even when they have been watered down. If these claims will be made anyway, what point is there in trimming our policies in a vain attempt to suit the opinion polls and the media? Why not go forward with a clearly defined socialist policy which we are committed to implementing when Labour gets into office? We have no need to be ashamed of our beliefs, or of our achievements. We should remember the words of William Morris:

'What is this, the sound and rumour?
What is this that all remember,
Like the wind in hollow valleys when the storm is drawing near
Like the rolling on of ocean in the eventide of fear?
Tis the people marching on.'

Let us continue that march, despite temporary defeats and setbacks. It is a new world we seek, the alternative is barbarism and ultimate destruction.

2

The 1974/79 Labour Government

I remember the General Election of February 1974 as a very cold affair. Canvassing and street speaking, which we do a great deal of in Walton, (we try to have a meeting in every street in the constituency), is better during summer months when the weather is warmer and it does not get dark before 9.30 or later.

The years of the Heath Government had been very active ones for me in the House of Commons. I had been involved in the struggle against Heath's anti-union policies and in particular had played a prominent role on Labour's Front Bench against the Industrial Relations Bill. That story I have told elsewhere in my book, *The Class Struggle in Parliament*.[1]

After Labour was returned as a Minority Government in March 1974, Harold Wilson invited me to become a Minister of State in the Department of Industry, working with Tony Benn, who was to be the Secretary of State. The other members of the Department were Lord Beswick, Minister of State, Gregor McKenzie, a Scottish MP, and Michael Meacher, MP, both Under-Secretaries. I had known Tony Benn for some years, and during the Heath years had spoken with him from time to time on the same platforms around the country and also at Party Conference. I had noted his clear move to the left in the Party, and realised he was a powerful, dynamic individual. I got to

---

1. *The Class Struggle in Parliament* by Eric S. Heffer. Victor Gollancz 1973.

know him well; I liked him, but did not always agree with him. I first met him in the House of Commons after being elected in 1964. Prior to that he had been one of those remote people that one saw at Party Conferences, as part of the NEC on the platform. He was then, to me, a somewhat distant figure, and remained so until after Labour's defeat in 1970. I did, however, have one serious conversation with him late one night at the Party Conference before Labour's defeat in 1970; I told him then that if the Government persisted in going through with its Incomes Policy, and *In Place of Strife,* we would lose the next General Election. He felt I was wrong at the time, but subsequently agreed that I was then much closer in touch with the feelings of the Labour Movement than he had been.

After the 1970 defeat, because of his experiences in the Wilson Government, his centrist position changed and he moved to the left. He became very active in the Upper Clyde shipyard struggle and supported the Fisher-Bendix workers' struggle on Merseyside and the Meriden motor-cycle workers in the Midlands. He opposed the Heath industrial relations legislation enthusiastically and gave his support to the miners' strike which was very influential in bringing the Heath Government down.

Tony believed that any socialist worthy of the name identifies himself or herself with the workers in industrial struggle. At the same time, he articulated broader political issues and as Chairman of the Party's Home Policy Committee on the NEC, he put forward policies which were later embodied into *Labour's Programme* and also in the Party's document outlining its industrial policy with the need for a National Enterprise Board.

Tony won increasing support amongst the mass of the Party membership, particularly after he became Secretary of State. The press increasingly lambasted him with shrill and intense attacks. Unfortunately they were often helped by some in the Labour Government's highest ranks who clearly resented his fight to get Party policy carried through.

My time at the Department of Industry was my first, and incidentally my last, experience in Government, and as can be expected it took a few days to get my bearings and some weeks to become familiar with the job. I was given the task of looking after regional policy, and Tony also asked me to chair the committee working on the White paper dealing with Industrial Policy. Amongst the civil servants on the committee were Allan

Lord, who later went to Dunlops, and Ron Dearing, now chairman of the Post Office. They were joined by Frances Morrell, Francis Cripps, Stuart Holland and Michael Meacher.

The Committee met regularly and when the White Paper was finished I sent a copy to Tony Benn. As far as I was concerned it contained everything that the Party had called for: an interventionist National Enterprise Board, which could and would extend and develop public ownership and greater control over the investment policies and locations of the multi-nationals. It was, however, written in Civil Service language. This did not suit some people and, after discussion, it was, as Michael Meacher put it, radicalised in language. I expressed the fear that by doing this the paper would be taken out of our hands by the Prime Minister and its contents would be changed. I was right. After Harold Wilson and other Cabinet Ministers had finished with it, it was emasculated out of all recognition.

In his book, *Final Term*,[2] Harold Wilson says, 'It was not until late July that the Department of Industry's draft White Paper emerged. As I had feared, it proved to be a sloppy and half-baked document, polemical, indeed menacing in tone, redolent more of an NEC Home Policy Committee document than a Command Paper.' He went on to say, 'A special committee of senior Ministers was set up under my chairmanship to mastermind its re-drafting, which quickly decided the document should be re-written. The final draft owed a great deal to Michael Foot, writing within the parameter we laid down. The section on planning agreements was cut down to size; the role and power of the NEB (National Enterprise Board) was strictly defined; above all, it was to have no marauding role. It should act specifically within guidelines announced by the Secretary of State which were to be made public. These provided, inter alia, that it could not go secretly into the market, whether directly or through nominees buying the shares of a company with a view to acquiring control, but had to follow normal Stock Exchange procedures.'

Although I felt that it was a tactical mistake to 'radicalise' the language in the White Paper, I was absolutely furious with the final result. All the important meat of the policy had been

---

2. *Final Term — The Labour Government 1974-76* by Harold Wilson. Weidenfeld & Nicholson and Michael Joseph 1979.

removed, clearly under pressure from the CBI and the City of London. I felt like resigning on the spot, but was prevailed upon not to do so, because it was clear we were heading for an early General Election. A resignation at that time would not have been understood by many people. I stayed on and fought the election as a Minister of State.

The White Paper which emerged from the Cabinet Committee undermined the powers of the NEB. As Harold Wilson wrote, 'It asserted the Government's belief in a mixed economy.' The paper actually said, 'We need both efficient publicly owned industries and a vigorous, alert, responsible and profitable private sector, working together with the Government in a framework which brings together the interests of all concerned.' It abandoned the concept of compulsion, an essential part of the strategy without which planning agreements were a farce. Only one voluntary planning agreement was established under the Act, once it was law, and that was in the coal industry. Tony Benn made one last effort to salvage some of the policy. Barbara Castle in her *Diaries*[3] under the entry August 2nd 1974 wrote '... I was late for Cabinet, in whose business I was too tired to take an interest. ... They turned next to the industrial policy White Paper, which I thought had been more or less agreed — but not a bit of it. Wedgie returned to his theme about planning agreements and regional aid, saying he must have a lever to influence the big companies. He brought a hornet's nest about his ears. One after another his colleagues turned on him, Harold Lever summing it up when he said he could think of nothing more likely to shatter the already fragile business confidence than the suggestion that the aid industry had been promised might be at risk. Mike (Michael Foot) said nothing. Wedgie fought on alone, saying at one point, "What is proposed is a major change in this Party's policy." And he accused Harold of going back on his Conference speech.'

Despite the emasculation of the Party's proposals, Tony and I felt that as the NEB would be set up under the new Industry Act, we should do our best to make it work, and use it to extend public ownership in the interests of creating employment. But the White Paper, with its doctrine of the mixed economy, pre-

---

3. *The Castle Diaries 1974-76* by Barbara Castle. Weidenfeld & Nicholson 1980.

empted joint agreement with the NEC on the contents of the Autumn Manifesto. The Paper could not be debated during the life of that Parliament, which was rapidly coming to an end, yet it defined policy on public ownership for the coming General Election. In this way Harold Wilson intended to limit the possibility of election scares on the issue.

Some of the Party's Manifesto proposals were still in being, but not in the form intended. I well remember that when the NEB proposals were mooted in the Labour Party's working-party, during the period of the Heath Government, I was unhappy with them. I thought we were being side-tracked from straightforward public ownership, that the proposals smelt too much of Tony Crosland's concept of only developing publicly owned companies in profitable sectors. Subsequently I realised that Crosland was not serious about even these ideas because he came out against any NEB development at all. I remain of the opinion that it is better to state, in advance, which industries will be taken over, as it means that the development of public ownership is more clear-cut. But there is also a role for something like the NEB and it is unfortunate that this has been lost sight of.

After the second General Election in 1974, I continued as Minister of State and was at least able to help regional unemployment through the creation of Development Areas, although the multinationals were unimpressed by what they considered chicken-feed inducements. I still had responsibility for the Industry Bill which by now had been drafted along the lines of the White Paper. I was given the main job of guiding the Bill through the Committee. This was not only a great deal of work, it became increasingly embarrassing as back-bench colleagues put down amendments to the Bill which often I fully agreed with but which, as Minister bound by collective responsibility, I had to resist. All in all, it was a miserable period for me. I knew the proposals on the powers of the NEB and Planning Agreements were not good enough, yet, unless I resigned as Minister, I had to continue to defend Government, or more accurately Cabinet, policy (Ministers below Cabinet rank had very little to do with policy decisions, except within their own department). The problem was a recurring one which surfaced again around the issue of supplying aeroplane engines to Pinochet's Chile. There had been a debate about this issue in the House during the period of the Heath Government and as a party we had opposed such

exports. Yet after Labour took office, the Government did
nothing to stop the engines and other military equipment going
to Chile. I spoke against this and, as a consequence, was threatened with the sack. Although I survived as a Minister without
giving way, I was very upset by what the Government had done.
We did, later, step up support for refugees and other positive
action against Pinochet and I felt my speech had at least done
some good.

The final straw for me was the issue of the referendum on the
Common Market. The Government had promised to re-
negotiate the terms and did so. We were committed to then
asking the people to say by vote, whether they wanted Britain to
stay in or leave the EEC. Although Party policy had been to
come out and at the time Heath took us in, some Labour MPs
had voted with the Heath Government. It was clear that the
Party was very divided on the issue. I remember during the
referendum campaign, driving through Harold Wilson's Huyton
constituency and seeing his local party campaigning against him
for a 'No' vote. I took the view that Ministers who were against
continued membership should have the right to appoint one or
two spokesmen who could speak against in the House. I wrote
to Wilson urging this course upon him. He did not agree saying
that whilst Ministers were free to speak against in the country,
only those in favour could speak in Parliament. This seemed to
me unfair and I told Harold Wilson that I intended to speak
against continuing in the EEC in the House. He replied that if I
did, I would be sacked. I decided to speak nevertheless. It was
by no means one of my greatest speeches; I think I was too
nervous because of the build up from the press and media.
Shortly afterwards I received a letter from Harold. I had been
sacked.

After that I stomped the country speaking at anti-EEC rallies
and receiving tremendous support. Although the referendum
vote eventually went against us, it should be remembered that 8
million people voted to withdraw, and the bulk of those were
Labour voters.

It was during this period that the Government presented its
White Paper on Public Expenditure. The resolution the
Government put before the House on March 10th, 1976 was
very cleverly worded: 'That this House, in rejecting the demand
for massive and immediate cuts in public expenditure which
would increase both unemployment and the cost of living,

recognises the need to ensure that manufacturing industry can take full advantage of the upturn in world trade by levelling off total public expenditure from April 1977 while keeping under continuous review the priority between programmes.'

It still meant cuts and left wing MPs decided not to vote for it. As a consequence the Government was defeated. The following day there was a vote of confidence and naturally all Labour MPs voted to keep their party in office.

Harold Wilson was extremely angry with the left over this defeat but in our eyes the Government was pursuing what was basically Tory Policy. Unemployment was already rising and a policy of cuts, including housing and construction, could only further increase it. The Tribune Group, which worked well together in those days, numbered some 40 members in the Commons. But in government circles the left had clearly been defeated. Tony Benn was moved out of the Department of Industry to take over Energy. After his departure our industrial policy virtually collapsed. Though the taking into public ownership of shipbuilding and British aerospace were steps in the right direction, without a full industrial policy, including the massive extension of public ownership, the economy could not be properly planned. Step by step the Labour government adopted monetarist policies involving substantial cuts in public expenditure.

Part of the problem was the difficulty the government had in finding a majority in the House of Commons. In order to remain in office, parliamentary agreement was reached with the Liberals (a policy which was never endorsed by the NEC), and concessions were granted to the Ulster Unionists giving them more than their fair share of seats. Towards the end of its life the Government became deeply involved in wheeling and dealing. The well-established policy, first agreed at the 1933 conference, stipulating that the NEC should be consulted as to what should be done in such situations, was entirely ignored.

The Government eventually fell after its position was undermined by trade union opposition in the so-called 'Winter of Discontent'. This resulted from a Government decision, strenuously opposed by the left, to set a 5% wages norm for the public sector. It was obvious that this would be resisted by the unions who mounted widespread strike action. Disillusion with the Callaghan Government was almost complete. Once again, a Labour administration had lost touch with its own supporters.

Speculation as to whether the Government would have acted differently if it had had a larger majority has been widespread. My view is that given the in-built conservatism in the Cabinet and the fight the right wing put up against party policy before the election, it is unlikely. Certainly the Government carried out many positive measures but it failed to introduce the socialist policies which large numbers of Party members and supporters wanted. Many felt that future Labour Governments would have to be far bolder in their approach, especially on industrial and economic issues.

The record of Labour Governments, and especially that of 1974-79, raise the serious question as to whether they can ever advance socialism in a wholehearted way. I believe this is possible but it will require a Party dedicated to changing society and a PLP which will not panic in the face of our political enemies. These are matters which I deal with elsewhere in this book. Enough to say here that my experiences during my period as Minister taught me of the necessity to change the Civil Service and to ensure that we have open government, and that Government Departments must be made into instruments of change on behalf of the people rather than deadweights structured to prevent change.

As Minister, the first thing I had to do each day was to argue with civil servants to get them to do what was required. Their emphasis was to tell me what could not be done, instead of what could be done to implement Labour's policy. At times, civil servants would gang up on a particular Minister and get their own Minister, if he was inclined, to oppose what the other Minister was doing. When I first became a Minister, I was told by one senior civil servant that Ministers were either tamed or they left. I took the latter course. Civil Servants were described by Peter Shore as the 'Permanent Politicans'. That is what they are, the elected politicans being but transient figures on the scene.

A serious Labour Government wanting to transform society and carry out its policies will have to tackle this problem through a system of advisers who are between the civil servants and the Ministers, but who are sufficiently expert to confront a bureaucracy which attempts to ensure that the status quo is maintained. Recruitment methods will also have to be changed with the lower ranks having more say in the running of the Departments.

3
Thatcherism and the Crisis
of Capitalism

There are those in the Labour Party, including close friends and comrades, who say that Mrs Thatcher is not important, that the policies of her Government would be pursued whether or not she was Prime Minister. That, I believe, is only partially true; the role of the individual in history *is* important. It was Plekhanov, the Marxist 'Father' of Russian Socialism, who argued that human history as a process expresses certain laws, but in doing so, does not proceed independently of men. History is made by men and women, who set the problems of society and then deal with them in conformity with the historical conditions of the epoch. Fichte correctly explained it: 'As the man is, so is his philosophy.' Mrs Thatcher is a product of the crisis of British and international capitalism, and her thinking reflects it. Her actions are guided by a basic philosophy, of counter-revolution, authoritarianism and aggression. As Plekhanov writes in his *Role of the Individual in History*,[1] 'Men make history, and therefore, the activities of individuals cannot help being important in history.'

Thatcherism is, therefore, a phenomenon, which cannot be ignored; but neither should we be mesmerised by Thatcher and believe that if only we could get rid of her, then all would be

---

1. *The Role of the Individual in History* by G.V. Plekhanov. Lawrence & Wishart Ltd. 1940. First published in Russia 1898.

well and Britain could revert back to the time of middle of the road Tories like Macmillan, or nowadays, Heseltine, Heath and Pym and others of the Centre-Forward Group. The days of welfare capitalism are numbered, Keynesianism no longer suffices.

The Thatcher leadership took over the Tory Party, with wide backing from the Party membership to fight the trade unions and to lead the counter-revolution against 'creeping socialism.' She and her colleagues are as contemptuous of the Tory 'One Nation' brigade as she is of Labour and in one sense, coming as they do from the same party and philosophical background, they are an even greater danger to her.

There are those in the Labour movement who refer to Thatcherism as fascism. This view is incorrect — it misunderstands the nature of both. Thatcherism has very definite authoritarian traits, exemplified by its use of the state apparatus against trade unionists and its creation of an embryo national armed Police Force. But it has not resorted to the tactics of the storm-troopers and the jackboot. A better description of what Thatcher stands for is 'Bismarckism in a British context', a sort of top-hatted fascism, with the trappings of democracy still intact but increasingly hedged in by anti-democratic legislation.

The Tory Party is a very old political institution. It has an unbroken existence stretching back to 1640, longer than any other British political party. A recurrent feature throughout this long history has been the Tories preparedness to make tactical, short-term concessions in order to protect their long-term position and the system they represent. The events around the Reform Bill of 1866 are a classic example of this. The Liberals had brought forward a Bill which was a very moderate piece of legislation. Despite this, the right wing of the Liberals rebelled and, in alliance with the Tories, defeated it. The new Government, a minority Tory administration, faced massive working class agitation, organised by the Reform league. Royden Harrison, in his book *Before the Socialists*, describes the huge demonstration which took place in Hyde Park, London in May 1867. As a result of such pressure the Tory government introduced a new Reform Bill which was better than the previous Liberal proposals, extending suffrage to households in the towns.

The importance of being prepared to compromise in order to

maintain power was well understood by post-war Tory Prime Ministers. After the Labour Government of 1945-51 a strong mood for change continued amongst the British people. The Tories realised that they had little choice but to keep the welfare state intact and implement measures to create employment. They were forced to pursue a modus vivendi with the trade unions, and to develop welfare capitalism based on Keynesian concepts of intervention by the state in economic affairs. Even Churchill, an unenthusiastic reformer, ended up giving his blessing to R.A. Butler's Industrial Charter, a document which attempted to demonstrate that the Tories, far from having a laissez faire attitude to industry, recognized that 'strong central guidance over the operation of the economy' was essential. Looking back through Tory and Conservative Party history there is significant evidence to sustain the claims from within the Party that under many of their leaders, Peel, Disraeli, Baldwin, Macmillan and even Churchill, theirs has been a tradition of reform and moderation.

That tradition has certainly been shattered with the advent of Mrs Thatcher. Her leadership coincided with a deepening economic crisis which made Keynesian solutions redundant. She and her colleagues responded in a thoroughly reactionary way. They challenged the ideas of state intervention in economic affairs. The Tory strategy document of October 1976, *The Right Approach* declared: 'The precise limits that should be placed on intervention by the state are reasonably the subject of debate in the Party.' It is well known today that Sir Keith Joseph stood down to give Mrs Thatcher a clear run against Ted Heath. Russell Lewis, in his *Margaret Thatcher — A Personal and Political Biography*[2], described their relationship: 'Politically more than just friends — they were extremely close allies.' It is therefore illuminating to note the views of Thatcher's closest political ally, just after her ascension to the Party leadership. Speaking at Upminster Keith Joseph said: '... Our industry, economic life and society have been so debilitated by thirty years of socialistic fashions that their very weakness tempts further inroads. The path to Benn is paved with thirty years of intervention, thirty years of *Government* intervention, thirty years of disappoint-

---

2. *Margaret Thatcher — A Personal and Political Biography* by Russell Lewis.

ment. The reality is that for thirty years, Conservative Governments did not consider it practicable to reverse the vast bulk of accumulating detritus of Socialist measures and socialist attitudes have been very persuasive.. .... We have over-estimated the power of Government to do more and more for more and more people, to re-shape the economy and indeed human society, according to blueprints.'

'I agree that there are limits to the good which governments can do to help the economy, but no limits to the harm ... the Second World War brought about a swing of the pendulum on which it came to be believed that government could do almost everything for everybody without infringing freedom of opportunity. I think public opinion has grown wise or at least wiser to the limits of what government can do for people, to the decreasing returns and counter-productive nature of government provision and intervention beyond a point.'

These views very clearly revealed what sort of a government Thatcher would head were she elected. It would break totally from previous Tory Governments, certainly since the end of the Second World War. Heath, Macmillan, Butler and the other 'One Nation' Tories were to be repudiated. The 'One Nation' idea was dead; now there was to be relentless class war against 'socialism' in all its forms, especially in industry. As Sir Keith Joseph put it: 'the blind, unplanned, unco-ordinated wisdom of the market is overwhelmingly superior, to the well-researched, rational, systematic, well-meaning, co-operative, science-based, forward-looking statistically respectable plans of the government ... (the) ... market order is not perfect, it contains within itself the source of constant improvement. It is a self-improving system ... and therefore needs no reform from outside itself.'

At one bound, with the election of Thatcher, the consensus Tory politicians were defeated. They were thrust aside by a leadership that rejected the word compromise and went all out for attacks on the working class. This worried some Tories who believe that the end of the road of confrontation will be the end of capitalism, with the election of a Labour Government which will adopt clear socialist policies. One of those who voiced such anxiety and still does, despite his role during the miners' strike, is Peter Walker. Annually, he goes to the Tory Party Conference to make the same warning. Trevor Russell in *The Tory Party — Its Policies, Divisions and Future* describes the position of the 'wets' in the following way:

'Capitalism has changed, and must continue to change. Many of the reforms it has experienced have been imposed by Government — and many more will doubtless have to be imposed in the future with the aim, as Walker says, of enhancing it. The alternative to change and reform is destruction, sooner or later. That could still happen anyway, at the hands of a fully fledged Marxist Labour Government — and there will be little any future Tory Government or Tory Party can do about that. What is imperative is that the Conservatives do nothing which can hasten that process. Some of them are aware of the danger; others, including the present party leadership it seems, have yet to grasp it.'

On the 25th February 1979, Mrs Thatcher, in an interview for the *Observer*, said, 'A future Conservative Government must be a conviction Government. As Prime Minister I could not waste time having any internal arguments.' In the years since then she has emptied the government of all those who have not gone along with her on fundamental issues. Ian Gilmour, James Prior, Francis Pym, Mark Carlisle and Michael Heseltine have all gone, whilst Walker continues in the Cabinet only because he was able to use the miners' strike to prove that despite his 'wetness' he is just as tough as Mrs Thatcher on the trade unions.

Many of those she has crossed swords with in her own party argue powerfully that Thatcherism is not really Toryism at all, that in advancing liberal laissez faire economic policies, it cuts across traditional Tory economic concepts. Of course, Thatcher genuinely believes that capitalism is best served by her type of policy. The ruling class are clearly divided over this question and are not sure which way to turn. This disorientation and division could be used to advantage by the Labour Party: When the ruling class is divided a united socialist party can surely gain. Unfortunately the Labour Party itself has developed a cracked note in its trumpet call, and shows divisions within its own ranks. Too often it is the Tories who take advantage of Labour's division rather than the other way round.

A central aspect of Thatcher's strategy is to play on selfishness, by encouraging individualism at the expense of co-operation and putting the self before the community. This emphasis, designed to split the working-class, is presented as part of a home-grown version of Toryism not influenced by the Manchester Liberals or Professor Milton Friedman of Chicago.

Sir Geoffrey Howe, in a speech at Hemel Hempstead on 30 March 1983, underlined this: 'One myth too must be laid to rest; that is the notion that our approach to Britain's social and economic problems has its origin in the University of Chicago or even the Free Trade Hall of Manchester. It does not ... The aristocratic tradition of paternal Toryism has a place, and an honourable one. But the Prime Minister's Grantham and my Port Talbot and the values and traditions which they bred, are just as much the cornerstone of what today's conservatives believe. Thrift, hard work, independence, the desire to succeed — not just for oneself but for one's family and country too — are now and always have been the moral bulwark of the Conservative creed.'

Howe is justified in pointing to a long line of those in the party for whom thrift and hard work are ranged higher in morality than matters like democracy or care through the welfare state. Let me give a few examples of what I mean: Sir John Wardlow-Milne MP wrote in 1932, 'The time has come for a complete reversal of the policy that children should be educated irrespective of any contribution which their parents may make'; Mr Austin Hopkinson MP held the view that 'The money taken from (the better educated sections) is distributed in doles to those who have no objection to becoming parasites, and breed like rabbits because they do not care what becomes of their children,'; and Mr Hely-Hutchinson MP, once said, 'I would take away the vote from those who had been in receipt of the dole for more than a fixed number of weeks in any year, restoring it when the recipient had been in steady employment again for a fixed number of weeks.' These were Tory MPs during the period of the National Government before the war. They were extremists, but they reflected a strong current of opinion in the Tory Party. There were Tory extremists in the House of Commons during the 1974/79 Labour Government as well. They used to sit in a group below what is called in parliamentary parlance the 'gangway.' They included Norman Tebbitt, Nigel Lawson, Rhodes Boyson and others, all of whom are either now in the Government or have been in it. As I write, one is Chancellor of the Exchequer and another Chairman of the Conservative Party. The extremists are now in control.

When in past General Election campaigns, Labour candidates have painted a picture of how bad it would be if the Tories were to win the election the predictions never turned out to be quite as bad as they were painted. Heath's Industrial Relations Act was a serious attack on the unions, but his U-turn in economic affairs is now famous. With Mrs Thatcher it was different. She repeatedly made it clear that she was not for turning. Her Government was, as Lord Kaldor wrote in his introduction to *The Economic Consequences of Mrs Thatcher*,[3] 'A truly ideological government of the right.' He points out that previous governments were essentially pragmatic without being wedded to any particular doctrine. They were more concerned with preserving existing institutions and traditions. Mrs Thatcher's Government ended all that. To quote Lord Kaldor again, 'They set about reversing the achievements of all previous governments since 1906 — relieving the taxation on the rich and well to do, putting heavy additional burdens on the low paid; curtailing the public services in all fields, apart from defence; imposing cuts wherever they could do consistently with their pre-electoral commitment and reducing the public sector by privatisation.'

That was the type of Government Labour faced and still faces. Because of this, and because of the disappointing performance of the previous Labour Government which paved the way for Thatcher's victory, the left in the Labour Party felt Labour's intervention had to be sharpened if it was to become an effective weapon in the fight against Thatcher. This, it argued, could best be done by increasing democracy within the Party and by ensuring that Labour's policies really would be carried out when it came to power. In other words, Labour must be as dedicated to advancing socialism as Mrs Thatcher was to supporting capitalism.

---

3. *The Economic Consequences of Mrs Thatcher* edited by William Keegan. Penguin 1984.

4
Extending Democracy in the Labour Party

There are those in the Labour Party who say that the years between 1979 and 1983 were wasted years in which the Party lost its way, that the people did not understand what it was doing and turned away from it. They refer especially to the constitutional arguments, and to a lesser extent the policy debates, which took place during those years. They mistakenly believe that these internal struggles could and should have been avoided.

It is important to understand what the basic objectives of the advocates of constitutional reform were and why the debates took place as they did. To obtain a better perspective some historical background is necessary. The struggle for the extension of democracy within the Party has been a continuous one. The history of the Party is scattered with such debates. Often these have been around relatively minor reforms but the demands for major constitutional changes in the period after 1979 certainly did not come out of the blue. As far back as 1975, I wrote for *Political Quarterly*:[1] '.. .... it could well be that some constituency parties who were dissatisfied with their Members of Parliament might invoke the procedure for re-selection. This is a right they have and one I certainly uphold. No Labour MP could possibly be an MP without being selected by the Party Management Committee supported by the

---

1. *The Political Quarterly* — October/December 1975, Volume 96, No. 4.

membership who work for them during election periods. The theory that an MP is above party and represents the entire electorate is a dangerous myth'.

But the debate goes back a lot further than that. The Chartist, Ernest Jones, included in his Election Address to the electors of Halifax in 1847, the pledge 'that I shall feel it my duty annually to present myself before the inhabitants of your borough, in public meetings assembled, and there to resign my trust into their hands, should such be the will of the people'. Perhaps this is not quite the type of re-selection the membership was calling for in the Labour Party, but clearly, amongst democratic politicians of the Left, the idea of accountability has been around a long time.

Constitutional changes were particularly demanded after the debacle and betrayal of the 1931 Ramsay MacDonald Labour Government. Then, even the PLP were moved to pass a resolution dealing with 'the procedure to be followed when the Party is asked to form a Government after any future election'. The motion, proposed by Walter Ayles of Bristol, called for a report 'with regard to the choice of the Premier and members of the Government' as well as 'the policy to be outlined in the King's Speech, and generally to be followed by the Party in applying National Conference decisions and handling questions on which no decision exists'.

The National Executive of the Party, which also accepted the resolution, issued a report at the 1933 conference recommending that 'after a General Election which has resulted in the possibility of a Labour Government, the final decision as to the steps to be taken would rest with the meeting of the Parliamentary Labour Party', but the PLP 'should have before it the considered views of the most representative body in the Labour Movement, i.e., the National Joint Council'. This Council, the report said, should consult the bodies represented on it, so 'their joint recommendation would be communicated to the Parliamentary Labour Party'. The National Joint Council was made up of the NEC, the PLP Executive and the Trade Union Congress.

Clause 9 of the report, said, 'Expenditure and finance generally should be a matter of Cabinet determination in relation to the general policy of the Government, and the Party should put an end to the practice by which excessive authority in this field has in the past been exercised by the Chancellor of the Exchequer'.

The report also stated that a Labour Government's policy should be based on Conference decisions and on the Party's election manifesto. The King's speech should, 'from year to year announce the instalments of the Party's policy with which the Government proposed to deal'. Because of MacDonald's betrayal it was decided that the Prime Minister should 'only recommend the dissolution of Parliament on the decision of the Cabinet confirmed at a Parliamentary Party meeting'. Most of these recommendations were subsequently ignored by Labour leaders.

It was the experience of the 1974-79 Labour Government, and particularly the way in which the manifesto for the 1979 election was drawn up, which rekindled the demand for significant constitutional change. I shall never forget the discussion on the manifesto which took place at No 10 Downing Street after the General Election had been called. James Callaghan, the then Prime Minister, flatly refused to include the Labour Conference decision, which had been overwhelmingly carried, to abolish the House of Lords. When pressed on the point, he threatened to resign. We, as the representatives of the NEC on the drafting committee, were placed in an impossible situation. Either we agreed to Conference policy being excluded from the manifesto or we had two elections on our hands. Amidst harsh argument the Prime Ministerial veto was applied.

It was because of these events that the demand for the manifesto to be drawn up exclusively by the NEC instead of by a joint PLP/NEC committee was raised at the ensuing conference. It was not carried, but other important changes were. Proposals were adopted for the re-selection of MPs and for a wider franchise in the elections of the Leader and Deputy Leader. In some respects, these proposals have turned out to be a mixed blessing but the principle of exercising democratic control over those who have been elected to leading positions was correct and should be extended further. Tony Benn has suggested that at some point in the future the Party should call a special conference to consider constitutional reform. This would be a modern version of the 1918 Conference when, for the first time, the Party openly declared its socialist beliefs and wrote Clause IV into its Constitution.

The argument has been made that the constitutional changes were brought about, not because of any great demand, but through manipulation by tightly organised groups such as the

Campaign for Labour Party Democracy. Undoubtedly, the CLPD played a very important role and organised in a very skilful way. But they could not have met with any success if the rank and file of the Party had not been convinced that an extension of democracy was essential. As Clement Attlee puts it in *The Labour Party in Perspective*[2], 'The Constitution of the Labour Party is inevitably the result of its history and expresses the balance of various forces which have created it.' I believe the struggle for the extension of democracy was absolutely correct. It was the only way of ensuring that genuine socialist policies are carried out by Labour Governments. In the future, MPs and Leaders will be accountable to the membership on a greater scale than ever before.

After the 1981 Party Conference, I felt that the left should not rush into an early contest for either Leader or Deputy Leader, entering instead a period of, to use the awful Morrisonian phrase, consolidation. I was unhappy, therefore, when Tony Benn announced his decision to stand for Deputy Leader against Denis Healey and John Silkin and said so at the time in a memo for the Tribune Group which was subsequently published in *Tribune*. I felt then that a contest could do damage, both to the Party as a whole and to the left in particular.

Obviously, once Tony's candidature had become a reality, I had to support him. The choice was an important one between two quite different political positions. Tony stood on a definite policy of carrying out the Party Programme and issued a statement on the 2nd April 1981 which contained four main policy commitments. The first priority was to restore full employment during the lifetime of the next Labour Government, by the adoption of the Alternative Economic Strategy. The second to expand and develop housing, health, education, welfare and other essential public services, both to meet people's needs and to create jobs. The third, to strengthen the rights of women, to extend democracy and self-government at all levels of industry, to defend the unions, protect the ethnic communities, to enact a Freedom of Information Bill, and to abolish the House of Lords. The fourth priority was to adopt a non-nuclear defence policy, to work for European nuclear disarmament and to secure the removal of all US nuclear bases from Britain. Tony

---

2. *The Labour Party in Perspective* by Clement Attlee. Victor Gollancz, 1937.

also said, 'We must strengthen the unity of the Labour Party and encourage the widest possible diversity of discussion within the spirit of tolerance and goodwill'.

As the campaign developed, it became clear that some Tribune MPs were going to abstain. Because I had not wanted a contest at that stage, it was suggested that I might join them. I made it clear that I would be voting politically for Tony Benn. On the 21st September 1981, the *Times* ran a piece by Christopher Hitchin headed 'The Left Jabs that could floor Tony Benn'. Hitchin made the point that if Tony won, the abstainers on the left like Neil Kinnock, Norman Buchan, Stan Orme and others, 'will look futile and (dreaded word) treacherous at the same time. If he loses they will be disowned as saboteurs ...'

As the campaign developed, Denis Healey and his friends began to scent victory. Some unions had a poll amongst their membership and one of the results which received wide press coverage was that of the POEU, in which Denis Healey got 56,768 votes, Tony Benn 15,660 votes and John Silkin 6,198 votes. The NATSOPA result was 12,948 for Healey, 4,496 for Benn and 2,129 for Silkin. The CLPs, however, remained overwhelmingly in support of Tony.

When the day arrived and the counting took place, the atmosphere at Conference was extremely tense. Tony was on the platform, not too far from me, and it was clear that the movement was reaching a historic moment. He lost by a hair's breadth. After the vote, it was found that 20 of the 72 Tribune Group of MPs did not vote for him.

The fury against those who abstained was awful to behold. The irony is that today some of those who fiercely attacked Neil Kinnock and the others, and who were really rude and brutal in their attitude, are the very ones who are today giving Neil unqualified support and denouncing those who have genuine doubts and criticisms of the way in which the Party is heading.

The re-selection of MPs was an obvious consequence of disillusion by the membership with the growing list of fifth columnists, people like Reg Prentice, Ray Gunter, Roy Jenkins and George Brown, to name but a few, who simply made use of their position in the movement before turning their backs on it. Clearly they had never really believed in socialism, yet they represented it and there was nothing real socialists could do about it.

Many MPs who have been selected on the basis of leftish-sounding speeches at constituency level, act somewhat differently when they join the PLP. They behave as an elite, ignoring the membership which elected them and the decisions of the Party conference. A classic example of this can be observed around the decision by the Heath government to enter the Common Market. Both the annual conference and a special conference of the Party called specifically to discuss the matter had clearly decided to oppose entry. Even the PLP, at a series of meetings had taken this position. Yet, when it came to the vote, the Deputy Leader and the Chair of the PLP, together with many other Labour MPs, openly flouted Party policy by voting with Heath. Such actions were never forgotten by Party members in the country although disciplinary action against those responsible was, in my view correctly, resisted.

The constitutional changes were obviously largely responsible for the departure of David Owen and others who left to form the SDP. They recognised that in future they would have to be more accountable to their local parties and their elitist attitudes would no longer be acceptable. They tried to confuse the issue by advancing all manner of proposals which, though at first appearing to be an extension of democracy, were in reality, merely attempts to deflect the party from the firm proposals under discussion. One such proposal suggested that the Party should adopt the US primary system of elections, that the selection and re-selection of MPs should be taken out of the hands of the CLPs, that representative democracy was not good enough, and should be replaced by proportional representation. This was a very strange argument, involving the use of list systems, where lists of candidates are drawn up by the leading committees of the Party, an arrangement which is, in fact, much less democratic than the existing system of selection by Constituency Management Committees.

All political parties, especially parties of the left, go through periods when renewal is a necessity. Parties become ossified, bureaucratic, too centralised and, as a result, less radical. The need for renewal is particularly important in a party which has as its objective the removal of capitalism and its replacement by a socialist system. But party organisation cannot be an end in itself. It has to serve the Party's political objectives. The best organisation in the world cannot bring results, if those in the Party are not convinced that it is going in the right direction.

Greater control and influence over MPs, the NEC and the Party leaders, cannot guarantee that socialist policies will be carried out. It can help by acting as a deterrent to those who would easily overturn policy decisions and conference resolutions, but it can never, by itself, ensure that they remain true to the basic principles and ideas of the movement.

There is never any great constitutional argument if people in positions of authority are carrying out the general wishes of the Party. Although the 1933 NEC Report referred to earlier was accepted and agreed to by the entire Party both Clement Attlee and Harold Wilson subsequently ignored its terms. Why then did the Party membership not rise up in revolt? The reason was relatively simple: Attlee, in 1945, was carrying out the policies the Party wanted. His government introduced the Welfare State, the National Health Service, and nationalised the coal-mines, the gas and electricity supply industries, as well as the railways. As a consequence, the leader did not come under too much scrutiny. The same was true of Harold Wilson. He had taken over after a period of intense disunity in the Party with Gaitskill leading a crusade against the left. Wilson with his speeches about the scientific revolution, with socialism as the objective, brought the Party together so that even his left critics felt it important to give him support.

The real arguments did not arise until the last years of the 1974/79 Government. By then the Industrial Policy had been abandoned, the Parliamentary Leadership had supported remaining in the EEC, a semi-compulsory Incomes Policy had been introduced, and the Government had allowed the IMF to more or less dictate the terms of its' economic policy. Just as after 1931, the party membership felt that something had to be done to safeguard the basic socialist ideas and principles of the Party. One only has to look at the Conference agendas of those years to see the upsurge of feeling in the constituencies and in some trade unions, about the need for constitutional changes.

Organisation is only important if it is understood to be complimentary to policies and principles. The Labour Party, in my view, is a socialist party, or it is nothing. Once it abandons socialism, once it turns its back on the class it was created to represent, it cannot continue to be regarded as the instrument of the working people in their efforts to create a new, socialist world. The constitutional reforms of 1979/81 were designed to ensure that the socialist policies and aspirations of the membership were put into effect, and were not betrayed or abandoned. They were attacked by the right-wing of the Party, and were constantly sniped at in the press. In order to counteract them, right-wing trade union leaders pressurised the NEC into the establishment of a commission to examine the workings of the Party. The Commission had three joint Chairmen, Michael Foot for the PLP, David Basnett for the Trade Unions, and myself for the NEC. It held a series of meetings which examined the structure and organisation of the Party in great depth and produced a report which was put before Labour's Conference and duly accepted. The Commission did not, however, get involved in detailed proposals for constitutional change, leaving that to the Party Conference.

This was by no means the first Party Committee to look at the question of organisation. It was preceded by the famous Wilson Committee which referred to Labour's organisation as being 'like a penny farthing bicycle' and also there was the Simpson Committee. There will no doubt be others — when a crisis of confidence takes place as a result of betrayal of policy, people look for answers in constitutional and organisational change. Such measures will never provide a complete answer. Equally important is that the party sticks to its basic principles and does what it says it will do. It is vital that the membership demand that the Socialist policies outlined in the Programme and Constitution are carried out, and that any constitutional changes are only brought in to ensure that happens. Individuals are important and if they fail to carry out the Programme on which they were elected they should either go, or a new mechanism for putting socialist policies into effect should be created.

5

Labour's Split and the Growth of the SDP

Writing in the *Political Quarterly* of October/December 1975[1], I had the temerity to say I was convinced that, despite difficulties which lay ahead, the unity of the Labour Party would be maintained. I stressed that as a left-wing Labour MP that was what I wanted. I also said I wanted to see the Party strengthen and continue its socialist programme. I believed that if the Party were split it would be caused by a small minority without mass support who wanted to turn Labour into a type of radical Liberal Party, or perhaps even something modelled on the American Democrats.

I was partially correct. The Party did split, but it was not a fissure of large proportions. Not one trade union, constituency party, or other affiliated body joined with the so-called 'Gang of Four', and this despite the fact that they received very wide media coverage.

At first, some thought that the SDP would be an attempt to create an old type Labour Party without a clear socialist programme. But David Owen soon made it clear that he at least did not intend to build a Labour Party Mark 2. He has been as good as his word. Today, the SDP proposes a 'social market' strategy which is very little different to the ideas put forward by Mrs Thatcher and Sir Keith Joseph. The 'Gang of Four' split

---

1. *The Political Quarterly* October/December 1975. Volume 96, No. 4.

from the Labour Party because they were convinced that, at last, a leading group of Labour politicians actually meant what they said; if Labour won the election in 1983, they intended to fight to get the Manifesto and Programme carried out.

In *Face the Future,*[2] published after the formation of the SDP in 1981, David Owen still talked in terms of being a socialist. His, he claimed, was an appeal for radicalism, not a plea for centrism which was a soft and flabby compromise. He even talked of eradicating poverty and privilege, and went so far as to say '... the present Labour Party can no longer claim to be the only vehicle for socialism in the country ...'

However, at the same time, Owen was repudiating basic socialist ideas. He explained that the Social Democrats would draw on the traditional conservative commitment to private enterprise and the market economy. They openly accepted the need for profit and would encourage investment and risk-taking. The radicalism he wanted was not the genuine radicalism of progress for the poor and downtrodden, it was that of the far right.

The SDP would like to go beyond the petty bourgeoisie for their support. Owen is aiming for support from the bourgeoisie itself. What he looks towards is the United States' system. He says in his introduction to his latest book, *A United Kingdom*[3], that in the USA, 'Government determines the services to be provided, which are then "designed" in partnership with the private sector through a contract franchise, voucher or other flexible arrangement'. He goes on with obvious approval, 'The significant contrast between the two (i.e. the USA and Britain), is that in the USA services employment has increased by far more than the decline in manufacturing'. Capitalism, therefore, is a good system, providing it follows the American pattern.

The SDP make much of their commitment to democracy. How, otherwise could they make their demand for proportional representation such a central part of their political strategy? Strange, then, that when they were inside the Labour Party they consistently opposed all the democratic reforms for re-selection, election of the leadership and so on. They knew that their own positions in the party were based not on the constituencies but

---

2. *Face the Future* by David Owen. Oxford University Press 1981.
3. *A United Kingdom* by David Owen. Penguin Books 1986.

on the trade union bloc vote at conference. Of course, after the reforms were accepted, Owen and friends made a dramtic U-turn and suddenly began campaigning for democracy themselves — in the shape of one person one vote. Their conversion to the democratic process had been quicker than Paul's on the road to Damascus.

On the surface, the proposal for proportional representation looks extremely democratic and fair. Today, there are people in all parties including Arthur Scargill and Stan Thorne on the Labour left, the Communist Party, as well as some Tory MPs who are in favour of PR. The SDP/Liberal Alliance makes PR an essential plank in their programme. If there were to be a hung Parliament, they would endeavour to extract concessions for PR from the Party in Government as a condition of support and maintenance of its term in office.

David Owen, in *A United Kingdom* writes 'The strongest argument for proportional representation is that the country has had sufficient experience of the present system with its unfair voting, adversarial politics and alternation of Governments to know that it does not work'. He argues that our present system 'has provided us with long periods of bad Government' and that Italy has enjoyed a higher standard of living because of its PR voting system.

The facts are not quite as Owen puts them. He admits, of course, that Italy has had forty-four changes of Government since the war and that under the British system, the Italian Communist Party would have been in office at various times. But he omits to mention that Italy does not have a National Health Service, its students do not get grants from Local Authorities, and the laws on divorce have only recently been changed. The truth is that, though Italy may have increased its standard of living, a left-wing Government could have made massive beneficial social changes, and assisted in the creation of a socialist Europe.

Owen dismisses the argument that the German Liberals, the FDP, are more influential than they should be because they only have a small percentage of the vote. The FDP, switched its support from the SDP to the Christian Democrats and has helped to turn the clock back in Western German politics. It is logical that the SDP/Liberal Alliance should support PR because they wish to be in the same position to determine policies and Governments, even though they are only in a minority position.

A favourite tactic of the SDP group has always been to invent policies on behalf of the Labour Party, and then insist that the Party reject them. I remember particularly their behaviour in this fashion prior to the last election on the issue of public ownership. I had helped draft the section of our manifesto dealing with this area and we had been acutely aware of the need to avoid creating large, bureaucratic nationalised boards and corporations. We specifically stated that public ownership would take many forms 'including workers' cooperatives, publicly owned companies, municipal enterprises, state holding companies, local enterprise boards and joint ventures between public and private companies'. None of this prevented David Owen from claiming that the NEC was only in favour of state nationalisation. His colleague David Marquand even went so far as to argue that the Labour left wanted an East European communist economy, something we had consistently and powerfully argued against.

Of the original 'Gang of Four' which left the Party, Shirley Williams seemed to have the most doubts about whether to go. I well remember that, as Chair of the Party's Organising Committee, I had a long chat with her in an attempt to persuade her to stay, but it was to no avail. Her recent book, *A Job to Live: The Impact of Tomorrow's Technology in Work and Society*[3] is well-researched and has much interesting material in it. But it is also centrally flawed. Williams warns of the dangers of the new technologies to people's livelihoods. She says in her conclusion that she has written about the way that '... the old epoch of the Industrial Revolution imposed itself on relations between management and workers, machines and people, and about the danger that we may repeat the experience in the new epoch of information technology'. What she fails to understand is that technology is a servant of the system in which it operates. Under capitalism it is designed to maximise profits and countless numbers suffer the misery of the dole queues as a result. But if production was for use instead of profit, technology could be used to benefit the whole society. Williams ends up with nothing more than a series of small-scale practical measures which, though many are useful in their own right, completely fail to

---

4. *A Job to Live — The Impact of Tomorrow's Technology in Work and Society* by Shirley Williams. Allen Lane, 1985.

deal with the central issue that technology is beneficial only in a society where the interests of the many are put before the interests of the few.

A constant refrain of the SDP is that there is too much confrontation in contemporary politics, or as David Owen puts it: 'Adversary politics continue to fan the embers of class politics'. This view is often bolstered by the media, and especially the radio, which frequently gives the impression that all MPs ever do is to sit in the Chamber and shout at each other. Admittedly, there is a lot of heckling in the House, especially at Prime Minister's question time on Tuesdays and Thursdays. But this is because, to a certain extent, the class struggle is played out in Parliament. The political parties are based on class divisions, and these divisions are real ones. As long as working people get sacked for speaking up for their rights or live in fear of unemployment there will be confrontation in politics and all the cant and hypocrisy of well-shod politicians like David Owen will not change it.

Without their alliance with the Liberals, the SDP would have made little headway. They are a party without any significant support on the ground and at by-elections are forced to rely on Liberal activists for assistance. However the alliance is a shaky one: in the Commons the two groups often vote differently from each other and are sometimes split three ways. They are divided on many basic issues like defence and nuclear power. The only thing which holds them together is political opportunism in pursuit of the balance of power after the next election. They would then attempt to make proportional representation the basis of their continuing support.

I strongly believe that in the event of Labour emerging as the largest minority, we should refuse even to countenance a trade-off with them but should go ahead and form a minority government which, if defeated in the lobbies, should go back to the country. Labour will need to be positive and strong to do this. There are undoubtedly many in the Party, especially amongst those in the House of Commons, who would prefer to seek an accommodation with the Alliance. When the Gang of Four left they had many friends and allies in the parliamentary party who stayed behind. Many of them are still there, in powerful positions in the Shadow Cabinet. These people are unashamedly right-wing and, like Owen before he left, are constantly making it clear that they do not approve of many of Labour's policies.

They are dangerous because they make real the possibility that the Labour Party could move towards an SDP Mark 2 type of politics. That would be disastrous, both for our supporters and for our electoral prospects. With the media support they will surely continue to receive, it is likely that the SDP will continue to be a nuisance to the Labour Party for some time to come. It is salient to consider the way the Democratic Labour Party split from the Labour Party of Australia and kept it out of office for many years. Here in Britain, socialists must mount an ongoing campaign to explain the nature of the SDP's politics so that the electorate realise that if they ever came to power they would show themselves as merely another breed of Toryism, without even a hint of proper socialist policies.

6
The Leadership Battle

The defeat of the Labour Party at the General Election in 1983 had a traumatic effect on the membership. Immediately afterwards there were those in the Party, mainly on the right-wing, who blamed the defeat on the policies we had advanced which, they said, were too socialist and frightened the people. This was the 'If only brigade', who harped on that things would have been different 'If only we didn't talk about socialism, if only we hadn't talked about getting rid of nuclear bombs and bases' and so on. For myself, I don't think it was our policies which lost us the election though no doubt presentation could have been improved. It was other factors that were at fault and some of these I outline below.

Firstly, for some time before the election, we had seen splits and divisions within the Party. A good number of the right-wing Manifesto Group had broken away under the leadership of the 'Gang of Four' to create the SDP. They openly repudiated Party policy on nuclear weapons, the Common Market, public ownership and constitutional changes. For this they received tremendous media coverage and undoubtedly caused a great deal of confusion amongst some Labour voters. At the same time, there was much talk in the media of the Labour Party being taken over by hard left extremists who would leave our country defenceless, opening the way to Soviet control.

Instead of confronting this rubbish, the Party leadership often pandered to it. Tariq Ali was refused Party membership, Peter

Tatchell was repudiated as the candidate in the Bermondsey by-election, and Militant editors were expelled. There were several on the NEC, including myself, who continually warned that all this was doing great damage to Labour's electoral chances but Michael Foot, who had been elected Leader because it was felt he would unite the Party on a strong left-of-centre basis, seemed to take no notice. I was disappointed in his leadership, though I felt I had to support him in the Shadow Cabinet against the pressures of Denis Healey and others on the right who were constantly sniping at him. Michael is a well-loved figure in the movement, who built a deserved reputation over the years for supporting those in the Party who were being attacked and persecuted for their left-wing views; it is all the more regrettable, therefore, that in order to maintain what turned out to be false unity, he found himself doing things which were the precise opposite of all he ever stood for. I am afraid Michael and I, although we previously worked happily together in the Tribune Group, had a number of clashes during this period. I sometimes think his socialism is tainted with a sort of liberal radicalism. This is compounded by an occasional inability to judge character so that he ends up supporting people because of their charm rather than their basic ideas and intellect.

The Party was also thrown into confusion by the Falklands war. On the evening before the special Saturday sitting of the 3rd April 1982 which debated the issue, I phoned the Secretary of the PLP, Brian Davies, urging that there should be an emergency meeting of the Shadow Cabinet in the morning before the Commons met. He told me he could not get hold of all the Shadow Cabinet members in time and therefore such a caucus was not possible; there would, however, be a Shadow Cabinet meeting after the debate in the House. I later discovered that some Shadow Cabinet members had met Michael Foot in the morning. Their discussions with him must have left a lot to be desired because in the opening of his speech he said 'It is a question of people who wish to be associated with this country, who have built their whole lives on the basis of association with this country. We have a moral duty, a political duty and every other kind of duty to ensure that that is sustained'. He went on 'The Government must now prove by deeds — they will never be able to do it by words — that they are not responsible for the betrayal and cannot be faced with that charge ... there is the longer term interest to ensure that foul and brutal aggression

does not succeed in the world. If it does, there will be a danger
not merely to the Falkland Islands, but to people all over this
dangerous planet'.

It was hard to conclude otherwise than that Michael was
encouraging the Government to send the Task Force to the
Falklands. Most of the speakers who followed endorsed his
sentiments. Edward Du Cann said, 'Let us hear no more about
logistics — how difficult it is to travel long distances. I do not
remember the Duke of Wellington whining about Torres
Vedras. We have nothing to lose now except our honour.'
David Owen concurred: 'The Government have the right to ask
both sides of the House for the fullest support in their resolve to
return the Falkland Islands and the freedom of the Islanders to
British Sovereignty. They will get that support and they deserve
it in every action they take in the Security Council and elsewhere'.

Labour speakers were few and far between and the only one
whom I felt spoke correctly and courageously was George
Foulkes, MP for South Ayrshire, who said, 'My gut reaction is to
use force. Our country has been humiliated ... However, I am
against the military action for which so many have asked
because I dread the consequences that will befall the people of
our country' ...

I was very disturbed by the tone of Michael's speech and said
so at the Shadow Cabinet meeting which followed the debate.
For this I was roundly attacked for being un-British by some
members; it was even suggested that my views bordered on
treachery. I did not take kindly to some of the statements that
were made, the jingoism was depressing, but I bit my tongue and
did not say all I felt. On reflection, I think I was wrong to have
held back. Mrs Thatcher used the despatch of the Task Force to
boost Tory morale and Labour played straight into her hands. It
was a difficult time, it wasn't easy to explain that opposition to
the war did not imply support of the military fascist Government in Argentina. But by jumping behind Mrs Thatcher so
quickly, we helped her to produce a chauvinist trump card at
the coming election.

The General Election campaign saw leading Labour figures
speaking out against their own party's policy. Jim Callaghan's
well-advertised speech against the Party's defence policy, which
he claimed would leave the country defenceless, had a disastrous effect and was, in my view, an act of political treachery.

All the press were at this meeting, even television cameras from the major networks. Callaghan was reported on every major news bulletin. The media did not find out about his speech by accident, it must have been distributed well in advance.

I get fed-up listening to people of the right, like Jim Callaghan, attack Militant supporters as enemies of the Party, when they themselves can make speeches like that, probably costing the Party millions of votes. Callaghan wasn't the only one — one or two things Denis Healey said about defence did not help either. Such speeches, especially when accompanied by SDP attacks from outside the party, surely confused Labour voters. I have always taken the view that in election periods one must swallow one's disagreements, provided that they are not around basic socialist beliefs, and concentrate on getting across the policies that can be supported without reservation. Some in the Party leadership did not do this in the run up to the 1979 Election and we paid the price at the polls. We were clearly disunited and this fact played an important part in the Party leadership contest which followed shortly afterwards.

The timing of the election for leader and deputy leader took the Party by surprise. On the morning of the day that Michael Foot resigned, the press were full of stories about his impending departure and his succession by the so-called 'dream ticket' (which others called the 'nightmare ticket') of Neil Kinnock and Roy Hattersley. I telephoned Dick Clements, Foot's aide, to express my concern about the way the matter was being handled. Clements told me not to worry, that the press reports were unfounded. He suggested that I write a letter to the offending newspapers explaining that Labour Party members would not accept their leader being selected by the media.

By lunchtime, Foot had announced his resignation. Within hours, the TGWU and ASTMS executives, who were meeting that day, announced the candidates of their choice, before they had even publicly declared themselves as available for election. The 'dream ticket' campaign was already rolling and to many in the Party the whole thing looked very much like a fix. Prominent trade union leaders had decided who would get the job in advance of the election being declared.

Initially I wasn't sure whether I should stand. By the time I had discussed the matter with fellow MPs and my constituency party members and decided to run, the campaign for the other candidates was already well underway. I knew from the outset that I did not stand a cat in hell's chance of winning but I wanted to use the campaign as a platform for our socialist programme. The statement which I issued on the day I announced my decision to stand outlined the need for a joint campaign with the unions to oppose the Thatcher government and explain the diversionary nature of the Alliance; for support of the basic ideas in the Party's constitution, especially Clause IV calling for the extension of public ownership, and of the policies agreed by Party conference on a strategy for job creation, nuclear disarmament and the creation of a socialist Europe; for an end to discrimination against women and black people and for the democratisation of the Labour Party so that the entire membership was more involved in policy making.

I asked Jim Callaghan, the Labour MP for Middleton and a good friend and socialist, if he would be my election organiser and he readily agreed. I approached both the Tribune and Campaign Groups for support. The Tribune Group decided not to make any recommendation at all though it was clear that with a prominent member, Robin Cook, as Neil's election organiser many would be supporting Kinnock. The Campaign Group, or at least most of them, agreed to back me. I needed their names for my nomination as without a certain percentage of PLP backing it was not constitutionally possible to enter the fray.

I have to admit that my campaign was not very professionally organised. Cash had to be raised to send out election literature and to pay for travel on election tours because there was, and is, no provision for financial help to candidates. Neither did the media give me an easy time. Some of the press, when I announced my canditature, attacked me for standing and I was even asked on television 'What right do you think you have to stand?' I have been around in politics for long enough to cope with things like that but it was unpleasant at the time.

There were four candidates in the election for leader — Neil Kinnock, Roy Hattersley, Peter Shore and myself. All were invited separately to speak at aggregate meetings of the Sheffield membership organised by the District Labour Party. The proceedings were broadcast live by the local radio station and cassettes of the speeches were made for sale. I was delighted to receive the votes of five out of Sheffield's six CLPs and it was regrettable, from my point of view, that such meetings were not organised all over the country.

As the campaign progressed I also received the support of a number of left wing journals including *Tribune Socialist Action, Socialist Organiser, Militant* and *Labour Briefing.* The Campaign for Labour Party Democracy threw their weight behind me and so did Labour Against Witch-Hunts. Tony Benn came out in favour of my canditature and his support was important. Having lost his seat at Bristol in the General Election he was not eligible to stand himself, though a year later, after the Chesterfield byelection, he would have been and many would have supported him. Some people have claimed that Michael Foot resigned when he did precisely because Tony was not in a position to enter the race for his successor.

In the course of the campaign I spoke on several occasions at meetings with Michael Meacher who was standing for the Deputy Leadership. He received support from the same quarters as myself but was also backed by many of Neil Kinnock's supporters. He often implied that, as a member of the Campaign Group, he would be voting for me as Leader but, when it came to the crunch, he cast his vote for Kinnock. I believe that some rather harsh words were exchanged in the Campaign Group as a result of his decision.

The outcome of the voting under the new electoral college at the Party conference was clear and decisive. Neil Kinnock won easily with Roy Hattersley coming second, myself third and Peter Shore fourth. Neil's victory was seen by most as a boost for the centre left in the Party. He was a member of the Tribune Group and, although he had not supported Tony Benn in the previous Deputy Leadership contest, he was known within the Party as a man of the left who was a close personal friend of Michael Foot and much influenced by Nye Bevan. He had gained popularity with the left at Party conferences by always taking the collection at Tribune rallies with knockabout, hilarious speeches. His timing was almost as good as Ken Dodd's, the Liverpool comedian. I remember once warning him, though, that he should try some political speeches and not confine himself to taking collections.

At the first available opportunity after the results had been declared I went to the rostrum and, speaking on behalf of the NEC, made it clear that our duty now was to help the leadership carry through Party policy and to work with them to win the next election.

In the Shadow Cabinet elections which took place soon after

we returned to Parliament I was elected in about 11th position. The rules of the PLP dictate that those elected to the Shadow Cabinet should automatically be given responsibility for shadowing a Secretary of State. It therefore came to me as a considerable surprise when Neil offered me only a junior post. I refused to accept it and when he offered me another, equally junior position, I refused that as well. On the following Monday I picked up my copy of the *Guardian* and read an article by Ian Aitken claiming that 'old stagers' like myself and Stan Orme were being put out to grass. I immediately telephoned Neil because it seemed to me, and incidentally still does, that the story had somehow come from his press office in an attempt to downgrade the left in the Shadow Cabinet. Neil denied any knowledge of the press story and claimed that he was very annoyed about it. Shortly afterwards he offered me the job of Shadow Minister of Housing which, though not a senior post, at least made use of my membership of the building workers union UCATT. Reluctantly, I accepted. I did not want to make a great fuss about the affair in public — it might have been interpreted as sour grapes or big-headedness. Nevertheless I was upset by what happened, especially when I reflected on the fact that Peter Shore, whom I had beaten in the leadership vote, was offered two senior posts as Shadow Leader of the House and Shadow Chancellor.

Throughout 1984 I was subjected to further attacks in the press. They claimed that I was the only awkward member of the Shadow Cabinet and that I sat 'sour faced' and uncooperative in the committee. I cannot claim that I was always good tempered during this period, I have a short fuse especially when I think that injustices are being perpetrated or socialist policies are under threat. I certainly did not agree with much that was being said and agreed in the Shadow Cabinet. However not once did I go outside, either publicly or privately, and attack Shadow Cabinet members or decisions.

The criticism in the press was compounded by a whispering campaign around the House. Because, during 1984, I was Party Chairman, I had to leave a fair amount of my work in Westminster to my Deputy on the front bench, John Fraser MP. He was always helpful and totally loyal and I did make time to work myself in the party's working committee on housing and in the Government Bills Committees. Despite this, the fact that I had asked John to share my burden was used against me in innuendos about my committment to the responsibilities I had been given.

Another rumour which went around was that I had favoured speakers from Liverpool at the Party conference which I chaired that year. Such nonsense was bolstered by a penicious article in the *Daily Mirror* on the last day of conference. Written by Peter Tory it was headed 'The Fiddler of Blackpool'. Jim Mortimer, then General Secretary, put the record on this point straight in his final speech and I took legal advice about prosecuting the *Mirror*. Subsequently the paper published an apology admitting they were wrong.

In the Shadow Cabinet election of November 1984, I lost my seat thanks to the decision by certain Tribune Group members to withdraw their support from myself and Tony Benn. It was only then that I began to air my fears about the perceptible shift to the right of the party leadership, a shift which accelerated during the course of 1985. The downgrading of the role of the NEC and the increasing attacks on Militant were, for me, signs that the leadership was squandering a marvellous opportunity to unite the party behind an all out attack on an increasingly unpopular government. The plaudits from the press, which had so roundly attacked me and others on the left, for the new style of leadership did nothing to reassure me.

7

The Role of the NEC
and Party Conference

Clement Attlee in his *Labour Party in Perspective*[1] wrote about
the Labour Party Conference: 'The final authority of the
Labour Party is the Party Conference, held once a year
regularly and on occasions more frequently ... The Labour
Party Conference is in fact a Parliament of the movement. It is
more, it is a constituent assembly, because it has the power of
altering its own constitution.' He goes on to say that the NEC
carries on the routine work of the Party through its sub-committees: 'Much of the work is done by standing sub-committees,
such as the Finance and General Purposes, Organisation and
Policy Committees. Questions of policy are dealt with by a
range of policy sub-committees dealing with finance and trade,
constitutional questions, the re-organisation of industry, local
government, agriculture, and other subjects. These Committees
co-opt prominent members of the Party with specialist knowledge, and investigate matters of policy and report to the Executive on the particular aspects of the Party's work with which
they are concerned.' As to the PLP he writes: 'Action in the
House is a matter for the Parliamentary Party, the members of
which decide on the application of Party policy. The Labour
Party Executive is the body to interpret policy between Conferences, but in its own sphere the Parliamentary Party is
supreme.'

Attlee's position is therefore very clear. The emphasis is on
the NEC and Conference to determine policy, and on the PLP to

---

1. *The Labour Party in Perspective* by Clement Attlee. Victor Gollancz, 1937.

carry it out. Nowhere does Attlee argue that policy should be made by the Parliamentary Committee, only that specialists in certain fields should be co-opted onto NEC policy-making sub-committees. That in theory is still the position, but in practice it is slowly but surely being changed. Increasingly policy is being drawn up, not by Party Conference decision, but by members of the Shadow Cabinet. In order to cope with this extra work, the Office of the Leader has expanded, so too has the number of Research Assistants attached to Shadow Cabinet members. These people are not employed by the Party, but now frequently find themselves co-opted as joint secretaries of NEC/ Shadow Cabinet policy making sub-committees.

Following the 1983 defeat there was a clear feeling within the Party that in addition to the main Committees of the NEC, such as Organisation, Home Policy, Finance and General Purposes, Youth, International, Press and Publicity, there should also be a Campaign Committee. This would act as a spearhead in developing a campaigning party. The committee was set up by the 1983 Party Conference which clearly envisaged it as an NEC statutory sub-committee.

The Campaign Strategy Committee that was finally set up is of a different kind. It has Shadow Cabinet members, and co-opted Trade Unionists, usually General Secretaries, so that NEC members are in a minority. It was quite clear that some people saw this from the outset as a Committee which would be central in planning and developing the work of the Party, by-passing the NEC. It would, as a consequence, be less accountable to conference. The Campaign Strategy Committee has as its Chair the Leader of the Party. This is not supposed to be a policy-making body, yet from time to time papers are drawn up by members of the Shadow Cabinet for it which, in effect, become policy documents. Though all the minutes from the committee have to be endorsed by the NEC, it often happens that they do not appear until after action has already been taken. Also working under the Campaign Strategy Committee is the Campaign Unit, which seems to have an almost totally independent existence. There is also the Campaign Organiser, Robin Cook, who is neither appointed by nor responsible to the NEC. This job, so we are told, only involves co-ordinating the MPs and integrating them into the overall Campaign work of the Party. But again, it seems another step down the road of taking policy organization and control away from the NEC and the Party

Conference it represents.

This shift away from the NEC has been justified by a myth, fostered by right-wing opponents, that the NEC of the early 1980s did not carry out effective campaigning because it was too busy passing lengthy resolutions and draft policy documents of an extreme nature which could never be acceptable to ordinary people. Neil Kinnock advanced this view when he was interviewed by Michael Charlton on Radio 3 in November 1985: '... The Labour Party and everything it stands for is consistent with the objectives and values as they're perceived by the British people ... except for a gap in relatively recent years when it appeared that we'd stepped outside those lines of comprehension.' He went on, 'In the two years, two and a half years, since the disaster occurred (the 1983 General Election), as the reward for three or four years in which we didn't take ourselves seriously and therefore you couldn't expect the British people to take us very seriously, there's been an immense change in the Labour Party, partly because of my insistence upon different directions, but also because the party has responded with readiness to a new assertion of what we stand for and the direction in which we should be going.'

To claim that the Party in the early 1980s did not take itself seriously is, in my view, a slander on all those who worked so hard in the Committees to prepare policy documents, and on the membership which, after careful consideration, endorsed many of them at Party Conference. If Neil Kinnock really believes that the policies in the run up to the 1983 election were so bad, perhaps he could explain what should have been omitted or amended in the 1983 manifesto. That manifesto was focused around an Emergency Programme of Action which called for, amongst other things, massive rebuilding of British industry; positive action programmes to promote rights and opportunities for women and ethnic minorities; substantial investment in house-building and improvement; more help for public transport; improvements to the environment; a new priority to open government at local and national levels; new initiatives to promote peace including the cancelling of Trident, the refusal to deploy cruise missiles, and the commencement of discussions to remove nuclear bases from Britain; the banning of arms sales to repressive regimes; an increase in aid to developing countries; and the opening of negotiations in order to prepare for Britain's withdrawal from the EEC, scheduled for completion within the lifetime of the Labour Government.

The Manifesto also contained policies which were not new, but which had been resuscitated from past years, and had been overwhelmingly carried by Party Conference. For example, it said that a Labour Government would 'take action to abolish the undemocratic House of Lords as quickly as possible and as an interim measure introduce a Bill in the first session of Parliament to remove its legislative powers — with the exception of those which relate to the life of a Parliament.' In addition it said Labour would 'Replace the present (Police) complaints procedure with an independent system accountable to local communities, with minority police representation' and 'would work towards the Party's aim of a 'common pension age of 60 and a 35 hour week.' It further said that Labour would 'return to public ownership the public assets and rights hived off by the Tories, with compensation of no more than that received when the assets were denationalised.'

The questions still remain to be answered: Where, in all this, was the Party not taking itself seriously? Which of these policies were beyond the comprehension of the British electorate? And if the manifesto was, as Kinnock seems to claim, so ludicrously out of touch with reality, why was Peter Shore the only person to openly raise doubts about its contents at the Clause V joint meeting which endorsed it? Of course, like all manifestos, the 1983 document was a compromise which included and excluded items that individual members may or may not have liked. But it is absurd for anyone to claim that it was not a serious document intended to provide practical, radical solutions to the problems besetting the country.

If the allegation that the programme prepared by the NEC in the early 1980s was unrealistic is unfounded, what of the claim that the same NEC was not concerned with developing campaigns in the Party? This, too, is quite untrue: One of the largest campaigns the party has ever organised, that against unemployment, took place during this period. Huge demonstrations marched through Liverpool, Glasgow, Cardiff, Birmingham and elsewhere. The Liverpool demonstration numbered some 500,000 people and had a tremendous impact on the city with Labour gaining substantially at subsequent polls. Another campaign, to defend the NHS was being planned well before the 1983 conference.

It is instructive, in considering the comparative campaigning strengths of the NEC and the new Campaign Committees, to look at their performance in relation to the most important campaign of 1984/5 — that in solidarity with the miners' tremendous strike. The NEC decided to throw their full weight behind the NUM and went to the membership to raise financial support. The response was magnificent, as I outline in Chapter 9. As to the Campaign Strategy Committee, not once did this body so much as discuss the miners' campaign, let along commit support to it.

Another criticism of the NEC during this period, made prominent by a couple of trade union General Secretaries, was that it was profligate with the Party's money. The AUEW, then under the leadership of Terry Duffy, went so far as to say that it would not give cash to the Party unless it was satisfied as to how it was to be spent. Again, these allegations are quite unfounded. Certainly the NEC spent money on improving the very poor pay of Regional Organisers, and it also increased the pay of staff at Party headquarters to bring it in line with that being paid at the TUC. A considerable sum of money had to be found for carrying out proposals from the Commission of Enquiry (set up, at the behest of right wing trade union leaders, to investigate changes in Party Organization) and also for the expensive move of Party Headquarters to Walworth Road, a move which I think was a good one. But in all of this, the NEC took great care in committing the Party's funds. Jim Mortimer and Norman Atkinson kept a very close watch on all expenditure and the NEC even asked Party staff to hold back on wage increases because of financial problems. The only time the NEC wasted money that I can recall was when in 1978 it was indicated by the Parliamentary leadership that the General Election would take place in the Autumn of that year. The NEC committed considerable expenditure to prepare for this, money which was wasted when the election was postponed to 1979. The NEC could hardly be blamed for that.

Such accusations of money wasting were instrumental in the setting up of Trade Unions for a Labour Victory (TULV). Initially this was formed by right wing trade union leaders. It collected funds for the Party but only granted cash to the NEC for projects it approved. Presumably it was designed to act as bulwark against the NEC but in this it failed because the left trade unions subsequently joined it and prevented it becoming a vehicle for right wing pressure. It was, in any case, unneccessary. If the union leaders wanted a direct say in what the NEC was doing they could have taken up the 12 trade union places on the NEC specified in the constitution. Nothing other than convention prevents membership of both the NEC and the General Council of the trades unions.

The power of the NEC has been further eroded by the creation of joint NEC/Shadow Cabinet Committees which develop policy and in which NEC members tend to be in a minority. These have replaced the old policy sub-committees of the NEC. I was centrally involved in those sub-committees, chairing those on the Middle East, Construction and the Machinery of Government (which developed policy for abolishing the House of Lords). They were highly effective bodies, well-serviced by the excellent research staff at Walworth Road and involving Shadow Spokesmen and MPs who had a special interest or knowledge of the subject. Care was taken to consider all views within the Party and unanimity around reports was constantly sought. The new bodies are less throughly constituted. Experts can be invited to give advice but such invitations appear to be increasingly selective with left-wingers being systematically excluded even when their expertise is unchallenged.

There have been big changes too inside Walworth Road. Towards the end of 1985, following a report from a committee which initially included Jim Mortimer and then his successor Larry Whitty, a major reorganisation took place. Whitty's report seemed to me to have originated less from the work of the committee and more from the minds of the Leader and new General Secretary. It proposed the division of the office into three sections, Communications, Policy Research and Organization, each under a Director. The position of National Agent was to be abolished and the other department heads incorporated into the three new departments. The International Department was to be abolished altogether with its head working under the General Secretary and its researchers subsumed under Policy. I would not argue that there was room for complacency in the Party Headquarter's internal structures, but these changes, which have now been implemented, further strengthen the power of the Parliamentary leadership over the party apparatus and weaken the influence of the NEC and the Conference. The abolition of the International Department is particularly to be regretted and can only mean that policy on such critical issues as

Latin America, Europe, South Africa, and so on, will be increasingly determined by the Front Bench in the House of Commons.

Pressure for changes in the Party conference is also growing. There are those in the party who think it should be less of a body of deliberation and decision making and more of a political rally, like Tory Party conferences, where Shadow Cabinet members are paraded to make speeches to the general public rather than dealing with issues raised in resolutions. Where conference is constantly breaking up into so-called workshops thereby dividing the delegates, and where video displays take the place of political debate. Such a development would be a long way from Clement Attlee's conception of the Party Conference as the Parliament of the labour movement.

The move of Party policy out of the hands of the NEC and towards the Shadow Cabinet has been slowly and carefully put into effect, without head-on confrontation. But it is no less dangerous because it is insidious. With it has come a marked shift to the right in the programme of the Party away from what Party members want and what will be neccessary to solve the country's problems when we are in power.

To see just how dangerous organizational moves of this sort can be, it is useful to consider what has happened to the Spanish Socialist Party, the PSOE. When Felippe Gonzalez took over the leadership of the PSOE, the party had a radical left image. Gonzalez argued clearly for withdrawal from NATO and the removal of US military bases and troops. But over the years Gonzalez changed his position on this.

At the 28th Congress of the Party held in Madrid in May 1979, however, the political concepts of the Party were discussed. Under the heading 'Principles', the political resolution placed before Congress stated that there was a class contradiction between the proletariat and the bourgeoise and that 'the PSOE reaffirmed its character as a class, mass Party — Marxist, democratic and federal'. Felippe Gonzalez had made it clear in 1978 that he felt the words 'Marxist' and 'working class' were inappropriate in describing the character of the Party and an amendment was put forward at the Congress proposing the deletion of that section. The amendment was defeated. The Left appeared to have the upper hand but Gonzalez promptly resigned as leader throwing the Party into confusion.

An extraordinary Congress of the Party was held in September 1979 to sort the matter out. Gonzalez and his friends worked very hard between the Congresses and the basis for electing delegates to the Congress was changed by involving regional rather than local groupings in a way that favoured the right. As a result Gonzalez was able to take power again at the Special Congress and the basis of the Party was altered. The left had been totally out-manoeuvred. Gonzalez went on to campaign with maximum vigour for a vote in favour of NATO in the referendum, obtaining victory against the votes of most of his party.

The slide over the issue of NATO was symptomatic of a leadership more concerned with image building than building socialism. Elizabeth Nash, in *Democratic Politics in Spain*[2], writes, 'The programme which the PSOE developed for the 1982 election campaign was not a particularly radical one, and did not figure prominently in the campaign ... The aim was to promise gradual continuity of change, without radical trans-formation to the left or right; to promise, in effect, little more than what the UCD had promised but been unable to deliver. The private sector of the economy was to remain virtually untouched and was to be supported by government policy to create the bulk of the new jobs ... The socialist programme won cautious approval from employers'.

Such a programme was sufficient to win Gonzalez a hand-some victory at the election but it does nothing to confront the basic problems Spain faces and the disillusion this engenders will be widespread. There is an increasing danger that the organizational shifts, away from the NEC and conference and towards the Shadow Cabinet, herald the same sort of develop-ment in the British Labour Party today. If it happens, we will find ourselves in a situation where Labour could win the next Election only to resist any radical change. Certainly any Labour government would be better than the Tories, but the type of government I want to see elected is one which will carry out the programme outlined in the 1983 manifesto. Only then can we avoid the disappointment which accompanied the Wilson and Callaghan governments.

We should recall the warning of Francisco Bustelo, a left wing Madrid Senator, against the right wing drift of the PSOE at the 28th Party Congress: 'If today we add a little water to the old wine, tomorrow we'll add a little more and in five years time there will be no more wine'.

---

2. *Democratic Politics in Spain* edited by David S. Bell. Frances Pinter, 1983.

8
The Shift to the Right

'The future of Britain is with socialist nationalisation and not with pensioner capitalism. Even ... Denis Healey's soothing reassurances about the (Labour) government's desire for a "vigorous, alert and profitable" private sector has failed to put a smile on the face of Mr Campbell Adamson (of the CBI). Mr Adamson knows — even if Denis Healey does not — that British governments have fruitlessly been trying to bribe British capitalism ... for forty years. Neither of these fundamentals seems, however, to have played a part in the budget deliberations of Denis Healey or the stratagems of Harold Lever who apparently believes that the City of London is a winnable Tory marginal ... While everyone in the movement apparently shares the belief that we should abolish poverty, homelessness, slum schools, hospital waiting lists ... it must now be clearly apparent that none of this can be achieved at the speed or with the breadth that we demand if we rely on capitalism to pay for it. Privilege will defend itself, and by that defence deny even the existing facilities to the underprivileged. There is no need to be apologetic about the extension of public ownership or the establishment of workers control. They are now prerequisites of the economic survival of Britain. If the Labour Government does not pursue with enthusiasm and speed the proposals for nationalisation and socialism entrusted to it by the whole movement, we shall relive 1970. There is no alternative in the capitalist system — it is a failure.'

Neil Kinnock MP (from 'Socialist Nationalisation' in *Labour Monthly*, December 1974)

In the previous chapter I wrote about the shift to the right that was taking place within the leadership of the Party. It could be described as a period of surreptitious revisionism; it is not so much a frontal attack on Socialist positions but a smooth out-flanking, slow but sure, that one day will reach a nodal point where we find the last vestiges of socialism gone and a total acceptance of the capitalist system similar to that of the SDP. Changes are being made which already indicate the direction in which the party is heading. There are clear signs that the social-ist content of policies is being watered down.

One major area where this is happening is public ownership. The Party has clearly pledged that industries which have been privatised by the Thatcher Govenment will be taken back into public ownership. However it is now clear that this commitment is being de-prioritised. As Neil Kinnock recently put it 'our absolutely predominant priority will be on generating employ-ment, production and investment so we can rebuild the British economy. Within that order of priorities, the use of funds for re-nationalisation will have to take their place in a pretty long queue'. This view was further developed in a statement during a television interview with Sir Alistair Burnett on *TV Eye* in February 1986. There, Kinnock stated that because of the need to concentrate available funds on relieving unemployment, Government action would be confined to ensuring that recently privatised concerns met their social obligations.

Kinnock's dramatic shift on this matter not only undermined pledges given by Labour Front Bench Spokesmen during various debates on privatisation, but clearly also went against a resolution carried on a show of hands at Labour's 1985 Confer-ence which said: 'Conference calls for their (the industries de-nationalized by the Tories) immediate return to state ownership after the election of the next Labour Government on the basis of the price at the time of purchase — and for this to be included as part of the Labour Manifesto'.

'Furthermore during the transition period of reinstatement of state ownership, Conference calls for charges to customers of essential services to be reduced to take account of the excessive increases made by the Conservative Government merely to enhance the share value.'

'In particular Conference accepts that British Telecom must be taken back into public ownership immediately on the return of the next Labour Government. This will protect services, jobs and British manufacturing industry, and demonstrate that privatised companies can be returned quickly and effectively to public ownership'.

'This Conference calls upon a future Labour Government to ensure that all major industries and services privatised by the Tories are returned to a form of public ownership, that is both accountable and responsible to the needs of its employees and consumers within a system of social audit.'

These policies had been subject to careful consideration by the Party. We had long and serious discussions about the type of compensation that should be paid. There were those who argued, at one stage including John Golding of the Post Office Engineering Union, that these industries should be taken back into public ownership without compensation. The waters of this issue were muddied by the way in which privatisation was carried through, with the sale of shares to workers in the industries concerned. The truth is, however, that only a very small percentage of workers purchased shares, no more than 2% at the most. The rest were taken up by the various institutions in the City. I believe, whilst we have to ensure that the workers with shares get a good and square deal, we could go much further than the current proposal that shareholders be repaid exactly the amount paid for the assets at the time of de-nationalisation. But even this position is being watered down. Whilst re-nationalisation is accepted in principle by the leadership, no time scale has been specified and the impression is being given that whatever happens it will be a long way off. This is designed to placate the City of London and the big shareholders but it is highly doubtful if it will have that effect. Even with a diluted policy, the big business interests and their Tory spokesmen in the House of Commons will still say that we are out to re-nationalise everything overnight in an unfair way. There is no valid reason, therefore, why Labour should not stick to the proposals in its Programme and be bold about what it intends to do.

Another area where established Party policy is under threat is employment. The Labour Party, throughout its history, has made full employment a major commitment. Keir Hardie, when first elected to Parliament, was dubbed 'the member for the unemployed'. When Parliament re-assembled in 1904 Hardie moved an amendment to the King's Speech regretting that there had been no mention of the need to create a Ministerial post with special responsibility for the unemployed. Following a Conference in 1906 in Liverpool on unemployment, the newly-formed Labour Party in Parliament put forward a commitment which had two principles: Firstly that every man had an inherent right to work, and secondly that the State was financially and morally responsible for the unemployed.

In 1907, Ramsay MacDonald raised, through the Ten Minute Rule, the Labour Party's 'Unemployment Bill'. It proposed the establishment of a central unemployment committee which would undertake to carry out a plan of national works and the appointment of local commissioners to effect this. The Labour Party, put up a tremendous fight over the issue. Pamphlets were written, marches were held, and agitation was carried out in every part of the country. Trade unionists were asked to support the Bill in a pamphlet issued by the Labour Party in 1908 which was called, 'The Labour Party and Unemployment'. It said, 'What have you to say to the Bill? You know that the unemployed man always threatens your wages. He increases the power of the non-unionists. He is constantly liable to become a blackleg. He drains your funds. You have now to keep him whilst the man whom he enriches pays nothing ... Wage earners! Stand by the unemployed and the Labour Party's Bill'.

The campaign continued through the decades to the end of the Second World War. The Party's Manifesto of 1945, 'Let us Face the Future', contained a section called 'Jobs for All' which commented on Labour's political opponents in the following way: 'They say, "Full employment. Yes! If we can get it without interfering too much with private industry". We say, "Full employment in any case, and if we need to keep a firm public hand on industry in order to get jobs for all, very well. No more dole queues, in order to let the Czars of Big Business remain kings in their own castles. The price of so-called "economic freedom" for the few is too high if it is bought at the cost of idleness and misery for millions". Ever since 1945, every Labour Manifesto has contained the objective of full employment. It has been a foundation stone of Labour's socialist concepts. Yet, again today, that objective is being compromised in Hattersley's shilly-shallying economic proposals.

Housing policy is also a vital area where changes are being pushed through without the approval of the Party. It has been argued by some in the Party that Labour's Housing policy at the last election, lost us thousands or even millions of votes, especially on the issue of Council house sales. The evidence for that is very scant indeed, though it may have had a marginal effect in some areas. Let us look carefully at what Labour said on housing: It began the section of the Manifesto on 'Homes for Everyone' by stating, 'Britain faces a major housing crisis ... Our aim is a decent home for all with real freedom of choice between renting and owning, on terms people can afford'.

With regard to council housing, the Manifesto put forward five points. They were that Labour would fund a national action programme to repair and improve or replace run-down estates; would strengthen tenants' rights on security, repairs and improvements, access to files, exchanges, transfers, and moves; would encourage more responsive and decentralised housing management and maintenance and promote tenant participation and democracy including housing co-operatives; would end all residential and other qualifications and extend 'priority' groups under the Housing (Homeless) Act; and would end enforced council house sales, empower public landlords to re-purchase homes sold under the Tories on first re-sale and provide that future voluntary agreed sales would be at market value.

The Manifesto also stated that Labour believes in home ownership at prices people can afford and pledged that a Labour Government would examine the ways and means of substantial financial help for first time buyers, with special consideration for council and New Town tenants. I cannot, for the life of me, see how the policies described above did damage to the Labour vote or could be unpopular amongst council house tenants, or those who were seeking to buy their own house.

I was Chairman of the Sub-Committee which drew up the Housing Document, 'Houses for the Future' which I put before Conference on behalf of the NEC. That document was in parts a compromise, and the most controversial part of it dealt with council house policy in a special section. It said 'In the context of a standstill in house building, huge reductions in housing spending and the deterioration of the public sector stock, the right to buy has only made matters worse; the best properties have been sold; and the remaining less desirable council stock has deteriorated through Government neglect'. It went on, '... we know that in some areas, such as the inner cities, the shortage of council houses and land to replace some council housing raises special difficulties. These could be considerable. In these areas local authorities will be free to determine whether, in the light of local circumstances, council tenants should be able to buy their houses. Council tenants who wish to buy a home on the private market would be helped by the more general assistance available to first time buyers ...'

With this important safeguard, I personally am not against local authorities building houses to sell, but the priority in areas where there are long waiting lists, and where people cannot afford to pay high mortgage rates, must be to build decent houses for rent. There are, however, those in Labour's ranks who have completey succumbed to Tory propaganda and now believe that council house sales should be allowed all the time, anywhere in the country. Unfortunately this view is held by some Shadow Spokesmen on the subject and they are pushing it for all they are worth. Here is another area where party members will have to be very vigilant if they want the historical commitment of the Labour Party to the provision of good public housing maintained.

Defence policy is held up by some in the party who feel criticism of the present leadership should be toned down, as the one commitment on which the party leadership will stand firm. The leadership will carry through our policy of nuclear disarmament provided we stay within NATO. With such overwhelming votes at successive Party conferences against nuclear weapons, it will certainly be difficult for the leadership to renege on our policy in this area. However I believe we should not be complacent about this. The pressure to change our defence programme after we have been elected will be tremendous. A repeat of the PSOE leadership's acceptance of NATO, despite years of opposition, could happen here in relation to nuclear weapons and bases. Denis Healey's comments to *La Stampa* when he stated that he was dissatisfied with our defence proposals and would be pushing for change before the next election are not reassuring. Neither are the recent reports of reputed meetings between him and Neil Kinnock to patch up a compromise.

An important element in the shift to the right within the Party has been the role of the Labour Co-ordinating Committee. Originally a Bennite grouping, the LCC now claims 1,000 members in the Party and has been key in delivering support from sections of the left to the new right wing policies of the leadership. The guiding principle of the LCC seems to be the maintenance of a relationship with Neil Kinnock. This has lead the group, despite its recently published 4 point charter which contains little with which those on the left could disagree, into a steady drift rightwards. As a consequence, many within the LCC have found themselves in new positions of power and influence within the official structures of the Party. But whilst the LCC may, at the moment, seem a good vehicle for those interested in furthering their own political careers, the path they are treading is not new and before long their so-called 'new left realignment' will find itself pretty threadbare. They cannot bask for long in the warmth of their past reputation as a genuine left ginger group, and as the memory of the old style LCC fades, so too will their ability to mobilise support at the base of the Party.

The scars of the 1983 defeat run deep; we received a fearful drubbing from the capitalist press and the entire establishment united against us. The reaction to this has been for some in the Party, including some who are supposedly on the left, to say that we must moderate our policy so that it seems acceptable to the media and the interests they serve. They say we should proceed with stealth, obtaining what reforms we can get here and there, but we must not make an all-out assault on capitalism and those who politically support it.

Those who argue in this way point to the relatively sympathetic press coverage which the Party leadership has received since it began its talk of new policy directions and its attacks on the Militant and others of the left. In this connection, the speech by Henry Albert Fear, an elderly comrade, who was given a Merit Award at the Party Conference in 1984, after 63 years' membership of the Party, is worth recalling. He said, talking about his father, '... he told me that the workers must oppose an economic and social system that makes (unemployment and poverty) possible. He also taught me my first lesson in party leadership; when the newpapers (we did not have television or radio in those days) praise your leaders, he said, "Watch them, they have to be watched because they are supporting the present system of society, which you are opposed to and which you have to change." He went on, "When the newspapers smear, revile and criticise and even condemn your leaders, they are doing the job for which you elected them". That comrades, is what I learnt at 14 years of age and it is as true today as it ws 60 years ago".

Keir Hardie, in *From Serfdom to Socialism*[1] wrote 'Latter years have seen the capitalist and commercial classes successfully worming their way to influence and power in the councils of the nation, and they in turn have surrounded their particular form of property — Capital — with the odour of sanctity and reduced the artisan to the same dependent position as the landless peasant. No law can give freedom to a people which is dependent upon some power or authority outside themselves for the necessaries of life. The owners of the means of life can dictate the terms upon which all who are not owners are to be permitted to live. This is the great new fact which socialists are bringing to the front. Socialism says to the worker: "It is not the State which holds you in bondage, it is the private monopoly of those means of life without which you cannot live, and until you make those means of life common property and inheritance of all you can never hope to escape from your bondage. The economic object of socialism, therefore, is to make land and industrial capital common property, and to cease to produce for the profit of the landlord and the capitalist and to begin to produce for the use of the community"'.

That, in essence, is the case for socialism. Labour's Programme today is its modern update. It is essential that we uphold the good, basic traditions of the Party because they are as true now as when they were first formulated. All backsliding from such principles must be opposed if unemployment, poverty and misery are to be eliminated. The membership can, I am sure, halt the drift to the right and insist on our full programme being campaigned for and, more importantly, being implemented once we achieve power.

---

1. *From Serfdom to Socialism* by J. Keir Hardie. George Allen (London), 1907.

9
The Miners' Magnificent Struggle

The miners' strike in 1984/85 was the greatest struggle of workers in Britain since the days of the General Strike in 1926. The Labour Party responded to it in two ways: The majority on the NEC and the mass of the Party membership gave it full support, but most of the Parliamentary Leadership, and some MPs, were lukewarm, and often privately hostile to Arthur Scargill, the NUM Executive, and even the strike itself.

The full measure of the leadership's opposition to the strike was not fully grasped until the Bournemouth Labour Party Conference, in 1985, after the strike was over. There, the Leader spoke against the NUM resolution, on behalf of the NEC. Neil Kinnock's speech not only outlined opposition to retrospective legislation, but also attacked the miners' leadership and therefore the strike itself. Opposition to the NUM resolution on the NEC was only carried by one vote and Conference itself corrected that, by passing the resolution. However the majority from the floor of conference was only small and it is clear that the miners should have been given greater support.

In Parliament much more could have been done throughout the strike. The PLP should have kept up a barrage of questions to Ministers and organised a series of debates supporting the NUM. Some MPs from mining areas, and a few others, did ask questions whenever they could, and took every opportunity to speak on behalf of the miners in debates on the economy and other matters, but this was done without the full backing of the

Shadow Cabinet. Stan Orme, within the limitations of his brief certainly did his best. But neither he nor anyone else on the Front Bench could give really effective support to the miners without the full backing of the Leadership. There were times when back-bench MPs were in despair (some who had given unqualified support to Neil Kinnock and Roy Hattersley) when points were put by the leadership in the House of Commons, on the issue of a ballot for example, which were not helpful to the miners' leadership, and gave sustenance to a hostile press.

The Party membership, however, was firm in its support. Throughout the country, either as individuals or as part of miners' support groups, they raised thousands of pounds, took miners into their homes, and did everything possible to help. The NEC urged all CLPs to raise money, either by a voluntary levy or by other means. It also called upon local Labour Councils to do what they could to help. The response was excellent, to such an extent that when Arthur Scargill, Peter Heathfield and other NUM Executive members met members of the NEC to discuss further coordination of efforts, Arthur was able to say that the Labour Party had raised more cash to support the miners than any other organisation of the labour movement. When I heard that I felt very proud of the membership, and knew that the rank and file of the Party were fully behind the miners in their great struggle.

It was the membership and the NEC, rather than the leaders, of the Party who observed Party policy in relation to the miners as outlined in the 1984 and 1985 Annual Reports and the proceedings of the 1984 Conference. The NEC passed a resolution in March 1984 which began, 'This meeting of the NEC supports all miners in their struggle to save the coal mining industry, and also expresses deep concern at the extent of the police operations in the current mining dispute which from the press, radio and television reports appear designed to prevent picketing at collieries. The right to undertake peaceful picketing is still upheld by the law, and it must therefore be upheld by the Police.'

In the course of the following year, until the end of the strike, the NEC reaffirmed its position several times. It went so far as to organize a joint meeting with representatives from the NUM Executive. It also ensured that cash was raised and arranged for NEC members to speak all over the country in support of the miners. I, a Chairman of the Party, marched with the General Secretary and the NUM leaders at the great rally held in London. It was therefore strange to read later criticism from some people, I think in the LCC, who said that all the NEC did was to pass resolutions. It did a lot more than that. It called for a joint campaign with the NUM to get across Labour Party policy on coal, but when the NUM asked Neil Kinnock to address a number of rallies, he felt unable to attend all but one, in Stoke-on-Trent on the 30th November 1984.

Why did the Shadow Cabinet and the Leadership not respond more enthusiastically to the miners' struggle? The answer must be that they were embarrassed by it. They took the view that the strike would lose the Labour Party support amongst the people. In this, they were surely wrong. The miners' strike did more to expose the nature of the Conservative Government than any other event since Margaret Thatcher was elected in 1979. It raised the consciousness of the labour movement and rallied behind it support which, after the 1983 election, had been on the wane.

It was widely recognised that taking on and defeating the miners was part of Thatcher's strategy for curbing the trade unions right from the outset of her stay at No. 10. The plan was outlined in the Ridley Report on the future of the publicly owned industries, a report which was given prominence before the 1979 election, and which was leaked to *The Economist.* Sadly, in retrospect, it was not given sufficient serious attention by the Labour and Trade Union movement. The report proposed that a future miners strike should be dealt with by building up maximum coal stocks, particularly at the power stations; making contingency plans for the import of coal; encouraging the recruitment of non-union lorry drivers by haulage companies to help move coal where necessary; and introducing dual coal/oil firing in all power stations as quickly as possible. The report said that the greatest deterrent to a strike would be 'to cut off the money supply to the strikers and make the union finance them,' and that there should be 'a large, mobile squad of police equipped and prepared to uphold the law ... Good non-union drivers should be recruited to cross picket lines with police protection.' It also advocated that the eventual battle should be on ground chosen by the Tories, on a field they thought could be won. All of these proposals were implemented by Thatcher's Government.

On June 7th 1984 Tony Benn, speaking in the House of

Commons, put the position very clearly. It was a speech that should have had the full backing from the Shadow Cabinet. He said, 'There has been a great deal of hypocrisy about the government not intervening. They are deeply involved. The police are preventing peaceful picketing. They have set up road blocks, introduced curfews in the villages and provoked on the picket lines. There have been cavalry charges against unarmed pickets. The magistrates have come in and introduced bail conditions that amount to a sentence — a sort of exclusion zone — for those who have been convicted of nothing. Much has been made of the crudity of the way in which the government have turned off every source of funds, including social security, to starve the miners back to work. They have deemed that the miners have been getting strike pay when in fact they have not. They have cut maternity grants and excluded from strike pay workers who have only been indirectly involved and were never employees of the NCB.'

What Tony described was a class war government, which used the State almost in its entirety to defeat the miners and to teach the whole working class a lesson. Yet when about 40 Labour MPs demonstrated in the House of Commons against Government policy in a perfectly peaceful way by standing in front of the Mace, we were attacked by the Leadership for doing so. Labour MPs were also attacked by the Leadership when they stood in their places demanding a debate on the miners' strike, a demand to which Labour's Front Bench had eventually to concede. When the debate did take place it was very beneficial to the miners' case and I believe led to a greater understanding of the true nature of the Thatcher Government. One thing I learned during the fight against the Heath Industrial Relations Bill, which had as its focus the debate on the floor of the House of Commons, was that because there are Labour MPs with real industrial experience on the shop floor, the workers' case is often well presented in Parliament. Again, I can only believe that the reason why Labour's Front Bench were not keen to have regular debates on the miners' struggle was because they believed that it would embarrass Labour, and because they were not really fully behind the miners in their struggle.

There was a time when it was said that government merely acted as the Executive Committee of the ruling-class. This was often dismissed as too simplistic but, in the case of this Government, it became reality. The Tories pretended not to be involved, yet they planned every move in the course of the strike. This was underlined when, at the Tory Party Conference in 1985, Mrs Thatcher made it quite clear that she had 'won', similar to the way she had 'won' in the Falklands.

There are a number of views on the role of the state in a Socialist society with some believing that under socialism the state will wither away and die, and others believing that the state will of necessity have to play a more dominant role. Where there cannot be any difference, however, is in the nature of the state in a capitalist society. The law is the means of oppression of the ruling-class over other classes and is not neutral. The miners were victims of the present capitalist state apparatus, by way of laws which defend the present capitalist system and Government. It is necessary, as socialists, to understand the nature of these anti-working class laws, and why we must explain the need for the capitalist state to be replaced by something totally different.

One hears today a great deal of talk about the work and views of Antonio Gramsci, the great Italian revolutionary. His views have been used by some people recently to suggest that he was not so much a revolutionary socialist, but a type of British Euro-Communist or a socialist revisionist.

I have been acquainted with Gramsci's views for sometime, first discussing them with Italian communist and socialist friends in the years following the second world war. Gramsci may not have taken exactly the same view as Lenin on the state, but in essence he accepted the Leninist view, and fully recognised the role of the capitalist state in oppressing the working class. Of course the state is more than merely an instrument of physical force to be used by the dominant class over the others. It is not just the army, navy, air force, the police, and the prisons. It is also Parliament, the Monarchy, and the various Civil Service departments who are responsible for all manner of state concerns. When a Government is in office which represents the dominant class in society, such as the Tories, it will use all the various parts of the State to perpetuate its class rule. That is happening today with the Thatcher Government, and that is why it is essential for socialists to argue that the present state apparatus, including the police and the armed forces, must be democratised.

The miners' struggle revealed more clearly than anything else for many years the real nature of our state apparatus. It shattered a lot of illusions. It also caused some in the Labour Movement to bury their heads in the sand, pretending that it was all a bad dream, and that it would have been better if the miners had not decided to fight for the future of their industry. The reasons these people gave for not supporting the strike centred primarily on the issues of picket line violence and the need for a ballot. The miners from the beginning of the strike suffered from police harassment, and from old and new laws. It was evident that the violence on the picket lines was due primarily to police provocation and action. Yet instead of this being properly explained, the miners were blamed and attacked by people in the labour movement. Violence was condemned on both sides by Labour leaders, but not by Mrs Thatcher who only ever blamed the pickets.

A national ballot had not been organised immediately before the strike took place and, as a result, Arthur Scargill was attacked as if he was a dictator and decided every action of the miners' union himself. In fact, the question of the ballot was magnified out of all proportion. It became with many, including some in the leadership of the Labour Party, a sort of Holy Writ, as if the strike was wrong and should not have been fought because a national ballot had not been held. Those who argued in this way were often people who had had no real experience in working-class struggle. They had never personally been on strike, and tended to look at the unions' activity as if it were a game played to a set of Queensbury Rules, instead of part of the class struggle. Once the workers were out, it was the duty of Labour people to rally to their support and to work for them. Unfortunately this did not happen and the miners' leaders were attacked. What Eric Hammond said publicly, and what Neil Kinnock said at the Labour Party Conference about the miners' leader, was being said behind their hands during the course of the strike, and the struggle was weakened as a result.

I believe that once Ian MacGregor had decided to attack, and the miners had responded by embarking on strike action, to have held a ballot would have paralysed the workers in the struggle. The NUM National Executive were quite right to decide at that stage to support the strike and call upon all miners to respond. Ballots are not always held when struggles take place. A ballot was certainly not held over the issue of the Falklands war.

The view is often expressed that if there had been a national ballot, the Notts miners would have taken strike action, even though they may have voted against it. There is no evidence to support that view. The position in the Notts coalfield has always been somewhat different from the others, based as it is upon historical circumstances. It was unfortunate that divisions developed amongst miners, but the NUM leadership, once the battle was underway, could not then surrender and call off the strike because some miners in Nottingham and a few elsewhere failed to respond.

What should the attitude of the Labour Party to industrial struggles be? Certainly, the Party cannot sit on the sidelines and be indifferent for that only helps the workers' enemies. It is my view that the Labour Party as a socialist body must support workers in struggle, and the PLP should give them full support in the House of Commons, not just as a tactic, but as a principle. It should expose the role of Tory class laws, and the role of the capitalist state, making it clear that such laws are not above society, and are the product of the class society in which we live. This was not done effectively by the Shadow Cabinet, because most of its members do not accept such a view of the law or the nature of the state.

At the 1985 Bournemouth Conference the miners asked that the Labour Party, once it got into government, should bring in retrospective legislation to indemnify the workers and unions who had been victims of the Tories' laws whilst the strike was going on. They also requested that there should be a review of all miners' cases. I personally do not think that these are revolutionary proposals. Other people in the past have received such support and the Tories have brought in a number of laws providing for retrospective action to deal with certain issues. Obviously one has to be careful about the use of this type of law and it should not be used on every occasion; but there are circumstances where it is fully justified, and in my view the miners presented just such a case.

The miners had fought for the entire working-class movement, and Arthur Scargill had been entitled to say in April 1984, 'The time has come to say to other unions, yes, we want your support, but not only financial contributions. When we are faced with Thatcher, MacGregor, the CBI, the Institute of Directors, we're entitled to say to colleagues in other unions: join us, come out with us in dispute.' Then was the time for action by the entire movement but union leaders, or many of them, not only did not respond, they did all they could to dampen down support. This was especially true for the electricians and engineers in the power stations, whose support could have been decisive.

When, later in the strike, the question of a General Strike was raised by Tony Benn and Dennis Skinner, it was too late. The opportunity of further union strike action had been missed. Some have argued that a General Strike could have beaten the Tories. It might have done, but with the present TUC leadership I doubt it. One should always remember the 1926 General Strike was abandoned because the TUC leaders were told it was unlawful, and because they were terrified of the forces they had unleashed. The strike was called off, at the very moment when its solidarity was greatest and working-class power was being asserted at local level. If that could happen in 1926, with TUC leaders, or many of them, on the left, and with ties with the Soviet Trade Unions, through the supposedly revolutionary Anglo-Soviet T.U. Committee, then today the proposal could not even get off the ground. It could only be a slogan raised at a time when it had no real chance of being carried out.

The unions should have taken more positive action at an earlier stage by increased blacking of coal etc., and if the law had been used against them, as it would have been, they should have ignored it. As action was taken against the union members, with fines and possible imprisonment, then the situation would have been transformed. But such action was never really contemplated by TUC leaders.

There is another interesting comparison to be drawn with the General Strike: the attitude of some in the Labour movement to Arthur Cook, the miners leader in 1926, and of others to Arthur Scargill in 1984/85. Cook was regarded by some trade union leaders, and certainly by Ramsey MacDonald as a real 'wild man'. Beatrice Webb was scathing about him. She described him as 'the Billy Sunday of the labour movement.' She further said '... It is clear he has no intellect and not much intelligence — he is a quivering mass of emotions, a magnetic sort of creature — not without personal attractiveness — an inspired idiot, drunk with his own words, demented by his own slogans. I doubt whether he even knows what he is going to say or what he has just said.'

Similar statements were often voiced privately amongst labour movement leaders who regarded Arthur Scargill too as a 'wild man'. Yet the true quality that the two men possessed was that they really cared for their members and were socialists who believed that capitalist governments had to be fought and capitalism ended. Arthur is basically a modest person. The important thing about him is that he is dedicated to the miners and the working class movement in general. He believes in socialism, and is prepared to fight for it. The entire bourgeois press has vilified him, making him out to be someone who is dictatorial. That is not so, as those who know him are fully aware.

A lot of lessons were painfully learned during the miners' strike. The NUM leaders for example discovered that the so-called socialist Government in Poland were only too happy to export coal to Britain and help break the strike. A letter from Arthur Scargill to the Polish Ambassador said, 'The NUM has no intention of even considering the 'offer' to receive 100 striking miners' children for a holiday in Poland because we are aware that at the same time as such an offer is made the actions of the Polish Government are directly assisting the Tory Government in Britain to do all in its power to smash the NUM and the miners' strike.' A message from the banned Polish trade union movement Solidarnosc, in the Mazowsze Region, dated January 28th 1984, said in part: 'The Government of the Polish People's Republic, despite hypocritical condemnation of the activities of the British Police in the columns of the regime's press by the regime's pseudo trade unionists, is profiting from the export of coal to Britain. It sells dirt cheap coal which has been mined in scandalously neglected working conditions ... the Polish workers' movement is at present not in a position to undertake practical action. But you may be certain that as you have supported and are supporting our struggle, so we are in solidarity with you.'

Arthur Scargill, like many other good left-wing Labour people, had previously midunderstood the nature of Solidarity, and had accepted the official explanation that it was a break-away union of an anti-socialist character. No wonder that on June 5th after the bitter experience of Polish coal, Arthur declared "I think I owe Lech Walesa an apology."

In conclusion, the struggle of the miners was magnificent; though they were starved and battered, they remained defiant to the end. They deserved the full support of the whole Labour and trade union movement but did not get it. They were let down by leaders of trade unions, and by some in the Labour Party. The NEC of the Party and the rank and file gave full support, but more could have been done, especially in Parliament and through a national Party campaign in the country. The leadership failed because it did not understand the nature of the class state in which we live, and the class nature of this government. It rejected the class struggle in favour of soft talk. The most important lesson that must be learned from the 1984/85 strike is that it is essential, slowly but surely, to build a truly socialist current in the Labour Movement, which will not shirk the fight on other occassions in the future.

10
The Bournemouth Conference

The 1985 Labour Party Conference at Bournemouth has been described by political commentators as a watershed in the history of the Party. For members of the NEC, one of the most important meetings at the conference took place on the Sunday evening prior to its opening. The NEC had before it the composite resolutions, as well as the statements and reports it intended to put to Conference. The two most controversial issues were the resolutions from the NUM and on Local Government, the latter dealing with the Liverpool and Lambeth situations. These issues had received wide press coverage, thanks, primarily, to Neil Kinnock. The press had particularly played up the NUM resolution which called for retrospective legislation to assist miners.

The debate on this issue at the NEC was long and at times fierce. At one stage in the proceedings the Party Chairman and the General Secretary were instructed to meet NUM Executive members to ask if they would consider modifying or even withdrawing their resolution. The NUM declined, pointing out to the NEC delegation that they had an obligation to those CLPs which had put down resolutions on similar lines to those of the NUM and then withdrawn them in favour of the NUM.

Late in the night, after much toing and froing, Neil Kinnock, who wanted the NUM resolution rejected, insisted that the NEC had to make up its mind. I agreed with that — the issue could not be fudged or avoided. I moved that the NEC support the NUM resolution and called for a recorded vote, which at that time was the perogative of any member of the NEC. The system has now been changed and recorded votes are only taken at the discretion of the Chair.

The atmosphere was very tense at the time the vote was taken. Some trade union NEC members only voted for the resolution because their Unions were in favour; they personally had no wish to go against the Leader of the Party. Despite this, the NUM resolution was lost by one vote. Michael Meacher voted against, causing quite a furore amongst left-wing NEC members afterwards. I was later accused by the press of calling Michael a class traitor. I did no such thing, but I certainly did not find his action to my taste, especially as he was a member of the Campaign Group of MPs which had given consistent support to the miners throughout the strike.

The NEC then decided, by a majority of two votes, to support a resolution from Sheffield on the Local Government fight against rate capping. The position was clear: the NEC would oppose the miners, but would lend its support to the struggle of Liverpool and other councils. Neil Kinnock took the unusual step, as Leader of the Party, of asking to speak on the NUM resolution. Clearly, he wanted the opportunity to publicly state his opposition to the miners.

The Parliamentary Report, always given by the Leader, took place on the Tuesday afternoon. I thought Neil's speech was going relatively well until, suddenly, out of the blue, he began to attack the Liverpool Labour councillors. His attack was not just against supporters of the Militant newspaper, but against the Council as a whole. Yet the Liverpool Council, as I show elsewhere, had merely been following Labour Party policy, as put forward by the NEC in 1984 and carried overwhelmingly by Conference. I considered Kinnock's attack to be grossly unfair and cruel, and I could take no more of it. I walked off the platform in a spontaneous gesture of opposition to what he was saying.

On the following day the press was full of praise for Kinnock's speech. Papers like the *Daily Mail, The Sun, The Express*, and *The Times*, were all saying how Neil Kinnock had now proved himself as a tough leader, someone who was fit to lead the country. They also suggested that his attack on the Liverpool Councillors should be but the beginning, that all Militants should be thrown out of the Party, as well as all those on the 'hard-left'.

Reaction to Kinnock's intervention by those groups who issue daily bulletins at Conference was predictable. The LCC, who generally give Kinnock almost unqualified support, sounded a cautionary note, but by the end of the week they were back on the side of the leadership. The Fabians openly welcomed the speech, praising especially the attack on Liverpool.

I have frequently been asked since the conference if, under the same circumstances, I would walk off the platform again. My answer is very simple: I would. At certain times in one's life, one's position must be made clear. I felt I had no alternative but to walk off and I would certainly do the same thing in the future.

Since the Conference, an atmosphere of witch-hunting has developed in the Party all over the country. In many constituencies, people are being singled out for attack because they have left-wing views. In Sheffield, a local Councillor has been expelled from Attercliffe CLP because he is a supporter of the Militant newspaper. The expulsion was upheld by the NEC, despite opposition from the Sheffield Labour Group who said he had been a model Councillor. Unfortunately, David Blunkett moved that he should not be given the whip because the NEC had agreed his expulsion. I find that deplorable. It is not only supporters of the Militant newspaper who are under threat. Party members have written to me from Exeter explaining that they were in danger of expulsion for publishing a paper called *Exeter Briefing*.

Obviously, many of those on the centre-left hope that such expulsions will be kept to a minimum. But the truth of the matter is that the right of the Party have got the bit between their teeth, and whether it is liked or not, the Left will be witch-hunted in ever widening circles. One member (an ex-Parliamentary candidate) in the Birmingham area has, at the time of writing, been refused a transfer from one CLP to another, because he has always been a Tribune supporter.

Neil Kinnock's speech gave a green light to all those on the right-wing who wish to carry out a left-wing purge. The atmosphere in the Party is now reminiscent of the days of Hugh Gaitskell. There is, however, one significant difference: Gaitskell was known to be on the right of the Party, whereas the present leader was on the left when he entered Parliament, a fact brought out in a recent biography. It is this past left-wing

mantle, now used against others on the left, which creates
confusion and makes it easier for the witch-hunt to proceed. I
fear that if the expulsions of the left continue, great damage to
Labour's electoral chances will occur. The capitalist press will
play up every disagreement and our image, rightly or wrongly,
will be of a Party split down the middle. We should not forget
the days of the SDP breakaway. The SDP took only a handful of
members with them. Not one CLP, trade union or affiliated
body left. Yet the events were portrayed by the press, as if they
had split the party from top to bottom. The same thing could
happen in reverse if the witch-hunt is not stopped.

Kinnock's speech was the negative side of the 1985 Party
Conference. But there was also a positive side, important for the
future of the Party. That is the resolutions which were carried,
on policy which directly contradicts the right-wing attitudes
being adopted within the NEC and the PLP. They prove that the
socialist heart of the Party is still very sound.

The 1985 Conference passed 27 resolutions, either by card
vote or show of hands, as well as some important policy statements. It is neither desirable or possible to reproduce them all
here, but it is important to register the type of decisions that
were taken. They give a clear picture of what policies the Party
membership want to see implemented by a future Labour
Government and the list is a substantial one.

Despite Neil Kinnock's attack on the Liverpool Council,
conference passed a resolution which 'congratulates those
councillors who voted not to set a rate in 1985 until the
Government restored the rate support grant stolen from their
authorities, and trade unionists who took action in their
support.' The resolution mentioned Lambeth and Liverpool
Councils specifically and went on to call for the NEC and the PLP
'to support and campaign wholeheartedly with Labour local
authorities and trade unions for non-compliance with these
unjust laws.' It also committed a future Labour government to
repeal the rate capping legislation and 'fully compensate those
representatives of the Labour movement who have suffered
personal loss, bankruptcy, disqualification or whatever as a
result of non-compliance with these laws'.

Kinnock was also defeated on the conference floor on issue
of support for the miners. The NUM resolution, despite NEC
opposition, was carried by 3,542,000 to 2,912,000. After paying
tribute 'to the heroic struggle of all who have been associated

with the miners' strike of 1984/5' it went on to call for re-instatement of sacked miners, a complete review of the cases of those in prison and the reimbursement of the NUM and other unions for all monies confiscated.

On a card vote of 3,639,000 to 2,680,000, conference carried a powerful resolution on the powers of the police. It called for the democratic control of police authorities by locally elected representatives, the rescinding of the Police Bill at the earliest possible opportunity, and for the setting up of an independent complaints body.

Oliver Tambo, the leader of the African National Congress, attended the conference as a fraternal delegate and a resolution was passed which called on the next Labour government to break off diplomatic relations with South Africa and impose economic sanctions until apartheid is ended. Interestingly, the resolution on South Africa that was endorsed by the conference was almost identical to a resolution which, when Tony Benn had presented it to the NEC, was opposed by some in the leadership as 'gesture politics'.

A resolution on peace and security called for a ban on all development of space weapons and demanded that an immediate stop be put on the deployment of United States missiles and their Soviet counterparts in Europe. Conference agreed that the Party would seek support from Western European socialist parties for the mutual disbandment of NATO and the Warsaw Pact.

At the end of the week, conference took its first ever debate on the issue of lesbian and gay rights. To the surprise of some, conference declared its opposition to all discrimination against lesbians and gay men, instructed the NEC to draft a lesbian and gay rights policy, and called upon Labour local authorities to take action against such discrimination.

These are just a few of the various important and thoroughly considered policies which the Bournemouth conference adopted. There were many others including new policy on overseas aid, homelessness, education, economic policy, transport and public ownership. Taken together they are an impressive testament to the strong socialist base which the party has in the constituencies and the trade unions. It is up to the left in the party to give prominent to these resolutions wherever possible, and to fight for them inside and outside Parliament so that they will be embodied in the Party's manifesto. At the 1985

Party conference the membership made very clear where it stood; now the leadership must be forced to base its activity around the priorities which were democratically decided upon.

It was unfortunate, but perhaps predictable, that despite conference's overwhelming endorsement of its radical socialist heritage, it was the attacks by the leadership on the miners and the Liverpool councillors which captured the headlines. And it was not only Fleet Street which found Neil Kinnock's unilateral declarations worthy of close and sympathetic treatment. In the November 1985 issue of *Marxism Today* Martin Jaques described Kinnock's contributions as 'liberating'. He made it clear that he supported the leaders attacks on Liverpool and his only criticism of what was said about the miners was that it was not said earlier, during the strike.

Jaques contribution underlines how far the Eurocommunists have travelled to the right. It was only the right that could possibly have felt liberated at what Kinnock had to say. Others at the conference were in tears, with anger and rage, at what they had heard. Jaques's article was, I am told, supposed to be 'critical'. The only critical part I could find was at the end when he wrote 'On balance, Labour looks a more hopeful prospect post- rather than pre-Bournemouth. It said a bit more of what it's not, though little of what it's for. Much here depends on the capacity of Labour's broad left to do some independent thinking and delivery; it is certainly not the time to lie low and "loyal". But equally it's not just their problem. For the broad left outside the party has hardly been strong on what we should offer in the 90s'. That last sentence cannot be debated; but if what Jacques has written on the general positions of the so-called broad left outside the Labour Party is the best they can come up with, then one thing is for sure: it is not a socialist strategy which is on offer.

11

The Liverpool Crisis
and the Labour Leadership

Merseyside has a level of unemployment which has now reached catastrophic proportions. In October 1985 there were 142,647 unemployed on Merseyside as a whole, some 21.5% of the population available for work. In the City of Liverpool 57,409 were without work and unemployment in the urban areas currently stretches up to 50%. In the summer of 1984 there were 1,300 school-leavers for every careers office job in parts of the county. Unemployment is particularly severe amongst the 8% of the population who are black — 33% are out of work. Young people are also badly hit with 41% unemployment amongst those under 25. Long term unemployment is on the rise; 53% of the county's unemployed have been jobless for more than a year. And worse is predicted: forecasters expect an average jobless rate of 30% throughout the county by 1990 with another 35,000 jobs disappearing in the same direction as the 60,000 that were lost in Liverpool alone between 1981 and 1985.

The human misery which such levels of unemployment bring is everywhere evident. The *Liverpool Echo* of October 1985 contained a report about a street in Birkenhead, Tees Street, which has been christened 'Dole Street' by the locals. Only one person was at work in the entire street, a blind man called Danny Doyle. He worked at the local dole office. Danny told the *Echo* 'It's a bit ironic that I'm working in the employment exchange. That strikes me as a bit of a sick joke'. He also said he felt bitterly sorry for the youngsters who were unemployed and commented 'As far as I am concerned the kids around here are great. They just need something to grow up for'.

Birkenhead is the home of Cammell Lairds Shipyard. At one time I worked there at my trade as a joiner, and in those days it employed over 20,000 workers. Today, that figure is down to approximately 2,000. The same is true of the Liverpool docks, where there were 25,000 dockers. Today, there are between 2,000 to 3,000. The ship-repair industry which used to be flourishing has disappeared altogether. After the war, when it employed 20,000 workers, there were dozens of ship-repair firms.

The jobs crisis on Merseyside is primarily due to the decline of the Port of Liverpool. Traffic through the port dropped dramatically when Britain joined the EEC; but even before then passenger ship services had virtually ceased and other trade had fallen steadily. The decline in the Port was accompanied by a collapse of manufacturing in the area. In 1984, of the 45,455 people employed in manufacturing jobs in the City of Liverpool, more than half were employed by just seven firms. The fragility of manufacturing industry is underlined by the City of Liverpool's Study, 'Liverpool's Economy':

'The "de-industrialisation" of Liverpool is nowhere more evident than in the City's manufacturing industries. Traditional industries like sugar refining, soap making, ship repairing, marine engineering and rope and twine manufacture have ended or are nearing the end of their long-standing role as sources of employment. Other industries transplanted in the early post-war period — rubber and synthetic fibre manufacturing — have also disappeared to become part of the area's economic history. In addition, while notable plant closures (eg. British Leyland, Dunlop, Tate and Lyle, Meccano and the proposed United Biscuit shut-down) have made a major contribution to manufacturing job losses, redundancies and natural wastage have been proceeding on all fronts, especially in what still is the City's largest manufacturing industry — food, drink and tobacco. In 1971 this industry provided nearly 30,000 jobs. This had fallen to 24,000 jobs in 1978 and to an estimated 11,000 jobs in 1984 — a decline of over 60% between 1971 and 1984 and 54% between 1978 and 1984. Nationally employment in food, drink and tobacco fell by nearly 20% between 1971 and

1984 and 12.5% between 1978 and 1984.'

Unemployment has not only been bad for those unemployed, it has also had serious consequences for those in work. It has resulted in low wages in many industries, especially amongst those workers not protected by trade union agreements or conditions set down by wages councils (which could soon be abolished by this Government). A pamphlet produced by the Low Pay Unit on Merseyside provides details:

'A total of a quarter of a million Merseysiders — nearly a third of the full-time workforce and three-quarters of part-timers — work for wages that fall below the Council of Europe's minimum threshold for a "decent" standard of living. Added to the widespread unemployment problem the extent of low pay has left around two-fifths of the Merseyside population living in or on the margins of poverty. Last year more than half (55%) of employers visited by the Wages Inspectorate were breaking the law — the second worst record in the country.

The problem of low pay on Merseyside has been getting worse, partly as a result of the combined effects of Government policy and the economic recession. Throughout the 1970s, male workers in the area earned above the national average. By 1983, their earnings had fallen to only 96.5% of the average. The lowest paid have suffered the biggest decline in their relative earnings.'

The despair felt by the unemployed, and especially the out of work youth, in Liverpool has to be seen to be believed. One can feel their bitterness, their increasing loss of confidence and their growing alienation from society. Drug taking has increased significantly, so too has petty and more serious crime. This is not because Liverpudlians are criminal or violent by nature. On the contrary, they are fine, friendly, helpful people who more than anything enjoy a good laugh, often at themselves. Many of the country's best comedians are from Liverpool and the arts in all forms flourish in the area. Many top pop groups have emerged locally from the Beatles to Frankie Goes to Hollywood. In October 1985 the premiere of a new film *Letter to Brezhnev* was held in Kirkby. It had been made on a shoestring by young working-class men from the town and went on to receive an award at the Venice Film Festival. Alan Bleasdale's TV series *The Boys of the Black Stuff* which depicted the plight of the unemployed on Merseyside was hailed by the critics. There are also many operatic and drama groups, painters, sculptors and poets producing very fine work in Liverpool.

Why is it, then, that with such rich talent to draw on, Merseyside economy and infrastructure is in such a mess? There are basically two reasons: repeated failure on the part of national government to address Liverpool's problems in a serious way, and a history of maladministration within the city. Since 1979, the Government has reduced the rate support grant in Liverpool by £360 million. In 1979 some 62% of the city's net income was provided by central government. By 1983 this figure had dropped to 44%. Following the 1981 riots in Toxteth, Michael Heseltine put together a package of help for the area. Though parts of this, like the Garden Festival, were of some help, it was in the main a cosmetic exercise which in no way dealt with the real problems. The Government, for dogmatic reasons, put its faith in private enterprise when what was needed was massive Government investment.

Liverpool has not always been a Labour controlled city. Up until the early 1960s it was dominated by a Tory vote based on the Orange-orientated Protestant working class. It was only at the 1964 General Election that Labour MPs became the majority in the city. Even then the Labour Party did not have a secure position on the council and the Labour administration in the town hall was shortly followed by a Liberal administration. The Liberals concentrated their main efforts on keeping the rates down at the expense of local services. Council housing for rent was not built, the emphasis was entirely on building houses for sale. Liverpool is still paying the price for these short-sighted policies as Michael Parkinson, the Director of the Centre for Urban Studies at the University of Liverpool explains in his important book *Liverpool on the Brink*[1]: 'The record of the Liberal Party in limiting rate rises caused enormous, if unintended financial difficulties for the City in the 1980s, when under the Conservative Government's new grant system, the City's spending record in the 1970s became the basis of cuts in financial support. Local ideological conflict over housing and spending in the 1970s sowed the seeds of national confrontation in the 1980s'.

---

1. *Liverpool on the Brink* by Michael Parkinson. Published in *Policy Journals*, 1985.

Parkinson's book, written from an independent standpoint and an important reference work for anyone who wants to understand what has really happened in Liverpool, goes on to chart the changes which have occurred in the City's Labour Party: 'From the late 1970s a new breed of activist began to join the Liverpool Labour Party ... They were younger, were willing to work hard, more committed, more ideological and often not members of the Militant Tendency'. He continues, 'The process of change was encouraged by other factors' and refers to trade unionists who had become politicised through the struggle against factory closures and moved left through general dissatisfaction with the Labour Governments of the late 1970s.

Labour took control of the Council in May 1983 and the Council, in co-operation with the District Labour Party, decided to fight the government over its budget. It refused to cut services and jobs and stated its intention of carrying out its declared programme of building new housing, sports centres and nursery schools. Labour explained to the electorate the scale of the problems it faced and displayed determination in doing something about them. The electorate responded by increasing its support for the party at the May 1984 elections. Labour obtained over 50% of the total vote in certain areas on a very high turnout for local elections. The people of Liverpool recognised that Labour had not invented the financial problems of the city. They understood that the Government had forced the councillors into a policy of resistance.

In the following two years Labour stuck to its promises. 2,600 houses were built, new parks and sports centres were developed. Thousands of construction jobs were created as a consequence. In an article in the Liverpool *Daily Post* of October 15th 1985 Alice Coleman, a housing expert based at King's College London is quoted as saying 'Liverpool is the pioneer ... The Labour Council are getting rid of the unsuccessful multi-storey blocks and placing people in houses with gardens'. Her view was supported by Lord Underhill, certainly no friend of the Militant tendency, who was moved to write to the *Guardian* after visiting Liverpool to say how impressed he was by the city's housing policy.

The role of Militant in all this is discussed in Michael Parkinson's book mentioned earlier. He describes the discussions which took place on the council over the level of rate to set in 1985. It was the group as a whole, and not just the Militant supporters within it, who were opposed to a massive rates increase of 20%. Parkinson quotes a back-bench Councillor as saying, 'I'm not a Marxist, I don't even believe in all this political stuff. I just don't think it's fair. And I wouldn't vote for anything but a 9% increase'. He refers to another non-Militant Councillor who had been involved in the disastrous election in the 1980 election after Labour had put rates up by 50% during the year they had been the biggest group of Councillors. He said he had wrestled with his conscience and had decided to oppose 20% and happily voted for the 9%. Another councillor, a successful solicitor who would be debarred from practising if he were made bankrupt, was told by his ward (which happens to be in my constituency) that he need not vote against massively increasing the rates. Nevertheless he voted for the 9% as he thought it right. Parkinson concludes 'Any political differences within the group between the Militants and non-Militants were overwhelmed by their unity on the issue. It would be the worst of all worlds to compromise in 1985, get accused of treachery and then find they could not manage on the money and end up in court anyway'.

In reality, the Liverpool Council is not controlled by Militant. But even if it were, those in office have been elected by Liverpool Party members and by the electorate of Liverpool and if there is a case to answer it should be raised by and answered to them. I know personally many of those who serve on Liverpool's Council. They are a fine group of socialists. John Hamilton, the Leader, I have known since we were young members on the Liverpool Trades Council and in the Labour Party in 1948/9. John is a teacher whose father was an active member of the NCLC and a founder of the AUBTW and could, I suppose be claimed as an early Marxist. He is a Quaker, lives in a small house, and has never at any time used his position as Leader to advance his own personal position. He is someone who it is a privilege to know and call a friend. Tony Mulhearn, the Chair of the District Labour Party, has developed over the years since I knew him as a young man, again on the Trades Council, into a capable working class leader, a very good speaker, and someone who is open, decent and sincere.

The Liverpool crisis has not been invented by Derek Hatton or the Militant Tendency and it has not been Militant but the entire Council who have been leading a fight against it. The unity of the Councillors has been magnificent and the basis of this unity has been Party policy, both national and local. It is all the more deplorable, therefore, that Neil Kinnock should attack the Council in the way he did at the 1985 Party confernce at Bournemouth. Kinnock made reference to the Council's decision to 'sack' its workforce. This was based on a tactic adopted by the Liverpool Council to hand out redundancy notices to all employees as a way of applying pressure on the government to provide central funding. Unfortunately this tactic was misunderstood and gave the Council's political opponents grounds to attack them. Trade union leaders and, even more regrettably, some left wing groups joined in the chorus of criticism which was not of a mistaken tactic as part of a fight to save jobs but of a council declaring widespread redundancies. Of course the Liverpool Councillors had no intention to sack anyone, their fight was to preserve jobs and services, as those who attacked them would have realised had they not been blinded by hostility towards Militant.

Kinnock's harsh words at the conference precipitated a critical situation which was only partially saved by David Blunkett who managed to persuade Derek Hatton to withdraw his resolution in favour of a composite from the Sheffield Party. Following the conference, Blunkett went to Liverpool to meet the leaders of the Council. It was at this meeting, which I attended, that it was agreed to establish the Stonefrost Committee. This was a group of financial experts who were instructed to look into the financial crisis in Liverpool and come up with possible solutions. The committee was lead, as its name suggests, by Maurice Stonefrost, the former Director General of the GLC. It also included Martin Pilgrim of the Association of Metropolitan Authorities (AMA) and the Treasurers of Camden and Sheffield Councils. The report from the committee was issued on October 29th. It proposed a series of cuts in expenditure and further increases in the rates.

Neil Kinnock seized the opportunity these findings presented to continue his offensive against the Liverpool council. He commented, 'Since the practical means of avoiding crisis and sackings now plainly exist, duty demands that the best combination of options is put into effect. The sums of money which exist or can be secured have not been invented by the enquiry, they were there all the time for those who wanted to look'. This statement was issued even before the Liverpool councillors had the opportunity of examining what Stonefrost had suggested.

Eddie Loyden, another Liverpool MP, and myself thought that this was quite wrong and issued the following statement on the matter on Wednesday October 30th: 'The report on Liverpool's financial position, drawn up by the Group of Local Authority Treasurers, G.J. Folwell, J.A. Marlow, M.G. Pilgrim and M.F. Stonefrost, and issued yesterday, 29th October, clearly requires careful consideration and hasty judgements and reactions should be rejected by everyone, and provocation by any source should be ignored. We are sure that all concerned with Liverpool's wellbeing and integrity will be pleased that those who drew up the report have given unqualified praise to Councillor Tony Byrne, Chairman of the Finance and Strategy Committee, and the Chief Officers of Liverpool City Council for the assistance given to them. They say, "It would have been impossible to produce this report in a few days without the assistance of the Liverpool City Council".

We would like to underline the words of those who drew up the report when they say "We have no doubt that all parties concerned with the future of Liverpool City Council, its services and the community, will recognise the need for a careful and quiet approach to the critical decision Liverpool City Council must take urgently".

It is therefore regrettable that the Labour Leader's Office should last night, at 6.30 p.m., issue a statement on the Report, even before the Liverpool Councillors had actually received it. It is also regrettable that a Labour Front Bench Spokesman on Environment should also appear on television, again before all those concerned had had time to look carefully at and study the report and all its implications. If the idea is to drive a wedge between Councillors, we believe such a plan can be counter-productive. Careful consideration is required, especially as the Liverpool City Councillors have been acting unitedly, and in line with Labour Party policy agreed by the NEC of the Party and by Labour's Conference 1984. For that they should be praised and supported, not attacked as if they were responsible for the policies of the Tory Government, which in fact they are fighting against.

At the Labour Party Conference in 1984, a Statement was put to Conference by the NEC entitled, "The Defence of Local Democracy, Services and Jobs". It said, "We therefore recommend the following policies.

1. Authorities should construct their budgets for 1985/86 in

accordance with local wishes — to protect services and jobs and to acknowledge the growing needs of those communities most hit by Conservative Party economic policy. Labour local authorities should not act as agents for central government even if the resulting budget is out of line with Government policy.

2. Labour Councils are asking for the return of the £9 billion of Rate Support Grant that the Government has undoubtedly stolen from them. They do not want to put up rates — they want the return to the authorities of the money needed to run their services. Non-compliance could lead to some Councils being unable to fix a rate. For others it could mean running out of money for essential services."

The idea was to build a joint strategy of all Labour Councils affected by rate-capping and penalties etc. Liverpool Councillors agreed to act with their colleagues elsewhere. The fact is that in the end, only the Liverpool Councillors stood united enough to continue the agreed Party policy. Others, unfortunately, divided ranks and the agreed strategy in most Councils had to be abandoned. Liverpool, for good or ill, decided to continue the struggle in line with Party policy.

It is not true, as has been suggested, that sufficient money has been in Liverpool all the time. The Report, in fact, totally vindicates the Council's argument that Liverpool is under-funded due to previous Councils and Government policy.

One of the important points made in the report is that some of the various options are available only because other local authorities can help to raise additional financial support for the City Council. Also it is agreed by those who drew up the report that they learned much about financial matters from Liverpool, and say it will be helpful to them to adopt some of Liverpool's financial ideas in the future.

Liverpool City Council Labour Group is not dominated by supporters of Militant Tendency. They have acted as a united body, and they are acting in the same spirit that George Lansbury (who became Leader of the Labour Party) and his fellow-Councillors acted in the 1920s.

As far as we understand it, Liverpool Councillors have never stated they would not increase rates. They did so in their last budget. We are sure they will seriously look at this report in a rational, intelligent way. They are as keen as anyone to get a sensible solution to Liverpool's problems, but rightly, as far as

we understand it, do not wish to place further burdens on Liverpool workers, rate-payers and industry. They need assistance,
not abuse, and much help should be given by all in the Labour
Party, based on Party decisions at Annual Conference.

We therefore trust that the atmosphere of charged statements
and continued press arguments will cease, and that the Councillors, together with all those concerned will be left in peace to
decide what should happen next.'

Unfortunately, the Council were not left in peace, and
although they finally raised the cash required, through a
Bankers' Consortium, they were not praised for it but strongly
attacked. Nonetheless the building programme was still underway and the jobs of all Council workers were safeguarded, at
least for the time being. At the same time, despite David
Blunkett's efforts, it became clear that the AMA Councils could
not really raise sufficient money to bridge the gap in Liverpool's
budget.

The Liverpool Councillors, whilst appreciating the efforts of
David Blunkett, said that if they were to put the Stonefrost
proposals into effect they would have to do many things they
had said they would not do. For example, rents would have to
be increased, so too would rates, and genuine sackings would
have to take place. As it stood, they could not accept Stonefrost
without going back on their word and this they did not want to
do. There was a clear misunderstanding at the Association of
Metropolitan Authorities meeting in London following Stonefrost and unfortunately tempers became frayed. Some harsh
things were said and because of that three Liverpool Labour
MPs, Eddie Loyden, Bob Parry, and myself, issued the following
statement:

'It would seem that yesterday's events at the AMA meeting in
London which some Liverpool Labour Councillors attended,
and which was undoubtedly an emotionally charged meeting,
with accusations being made against them by some people
which the Councillors felt were untrue and demands made upon
them which they at that stage could not fulfil without consultation with the Labour Party members in Liverpool, has led to
some leading people in the Labour Party over-reacting.

As we understand it, after consultation with Liverpool
Labour Councillors amongst the local leadership and with
others, the AMA proposals have not been rejected, although
some feel they do not in any way solve Liverpool's basic prob-

lems, which are due to under-funding by the Government over a number of years together with failure to deal with the City's problems by previous Liberal/Tory administrations. It should be remembered that in 1980 when Labour had for a year a minority administration they attempted partially to deal with the problems by putting rates up by 50%.

The Liverpool Labour Councillors have acted within the terms of the Labour Party's policy agreed at the 1984 Party Conference, "Defence of Democracy, Services and Jobs", which said that the policy of non-compliance with Government policy could lead to some Councils being unable to fix a rate and, for others, running out of money for essential services'.

In light of conference policy one might have thought that the Liverpool Councillors could have looked to the entire labour movement for support in their fight against Government policy. The reality was somewhat different. At the NEC on the 27th November 1985 a resolution was put forward by David Blunkett calling for the General Secretary to carry out an assessment of the situation in Liverpool. An amendment was moved by Tom Sawyer which called for an NEC investigation of the Liverpool City party to be carried out and for the party to be suspended immediately. David Blunkett accepted the amendment. On a recorded vote the resolution was carried. It was, in my view, a very important decision for the future of the Labour Party and, because of its importance, I give below the resolution in its entirety. I moved the deletion of the last paragraph but lost with only 7 votes. The resolution which was carried by 21 votes for, 5 against, said:

'The NEC, mindful of the resolutions passed in May and October 1985 in respect of Local Government action in confronting central Government on their policies of enforcing cuts in jobs and services, notes the decision of Liverpool City Council Finance Committee announced on Monday, expresses the hope that this will result in the protection of services, jobs and the housebuilding programme and congratulates all those sections of the Labour and Trade Union movements who contributed to finding a solution which did not put at risk the people of the city or the standing of the Labour Party.

The NEC notes in particular those parts of the Stonefrost report which highlighted the part played by previous Liberal/ Tory regimes in Liverpool, which contributed to the financial difficulties of that City since the mid-seventies, and the particular responsibility of the Conservative Government. In line with Conference statements and NEC resolutions, the Government is charged with complete indifference to the plight of its citizens and the results of their own policies towards the most deprived and desperate inner city areas. As identified in the Stonefrost report, the Government have failed to acknowledge and meet the needs of Liverpool and other similar hard hit areas, and have chosen instead to let others cope with the consequences.

In view of the statements made by some Councillors and Party members in Liverpool, the accusations and charges levelled against the Party, the trade unions and others, and the damaging and deliberately provocative nature of the attacks made through the media, the NEC resolves that an urgent examination be carried out by the General Secretary and eight members of the NEC into the procedures and practices of the Liverpool District Labour Party, and that, pending this report, no meetings or activities of either the District Labour Party or its Executive should be held.'

The Liverpool City Council Group countered the NEC decision with a resolution which began by stating that:

'This Labour Group condemns and denounces the decision of the NEC to hold an inquiry into the Liverpool District Labour Party and to suspend the District Labour Party pending the result of the inquiry. The Group finds the decision to suspend the DLP pending the result of the inquiry particularly offensive and an affront to natural justice.

We further condemn the calls for expulsions from the Labour Party of three of our Councillors and declare that the Labour Group will not accept the expulsion of Comrades Hatton, Byrne and Mulhearn or any of the 49 Councillors, who have stood by pledges given to the people of Liverpool, and we will continue to recognise them as Labour Councillors and Party members.'

The resolution concluded:

'We demand that the inquiry, having been established, be open to be seen to be fair and we remain totally confident that the conduct of the DLP will be vindicated ... We applaud the decision taken by the District Labour Party and by the Labour Group in defending jobs and services, a policy which has resulted in Labour now controlling 82% of parliamentary seats and highest local Labour vote since the war. Experience has shown that Liverpool District Labour Party is one of the most democratic and vigorous parties in Britain.

We further note and applaud the decisions of the T&GWU General Executive and the London Labour Party Executive to oppose witch-hunts and expulsions. We therefore call upon the Labour Party National Executive Committee to lift the suspension of the District Labour Party and to conduct the inquiry in an open and fair manner. Above all we call upon the national leadership to concentrate their energies in fighting the Tories and in ensuring the return of Labour candidates in the local elections in May.'

The weekend following the decision to set up the enquiry and suspend the Party was awful. The press was full of details that had never been discussed at the NEC: that hearings would be heard in 'safe houses', that people giving evidence would be 'guaranteed anonymity', and that evidence would be 'forwarded to the police'. It was alleged that some of this information had been given to the press by senior officials within the Labour Party and it appeared to me that Party members in Liverpool were being found guilty even before the investigation had commenced.

I put these points in a letter to Larry Whitty on December 2nd in which I also asked for assurances that the investigation would be open, with charges laid out on the table clearly and without anonymous witnesses or secret dossiers. It wasn't until February 2nd that I received the following reply:

Dear Eric,

LIVERPOOL

Thank you for your letters concerning Liverpool. Can I make the following comment.

Firstly, I deeply regret and am appalled by the press coverage. I hope you will accept my assurance that neither I or this office have spoken to the press on this issue. It is quite clear that none of the text of the report was leaked. That I hope indicates a degree of security at this end.

Secondly, whilst I am as anxious as you to avoid damaging splits in the Party, as General Secretary I am bound by the decision of the 1982 Conference and 1983 Executive decision endorsed by conference in relation to the 'Militant', and I am bound to carry out the investigation required by the Executive. I am aware, of course, that you opposed both those decisions, but I am obliged to follow it through. You will shortly be receiving a copy of the report. Frankly, there are substantial problems in the Party in Liverpool which need to be put right. The involvement of the 'Militant Tendency' is one dimension to those problems. I hope we can deal with that situation with the minimum divisive effect on the Party as a whole.

Yours sincerely,

J.L. Whitty,
General Secretary

On the 6th December, the Liverpool City Council Group called a meeting at the Liverpool Polytechnic where Tony Benn and I both spoke. Because of the importance of that meeting and the issues raised, I think it important that extracts from both speeches are recorded. I began 'The resolution carried by the NEC on 27th November said that statements, accusations and charges had been made by Councillors and Liverpool Party members against the Party, trade unions and others. I dispute that. Certainly, some individuals were named in not too flattering tones after they had made derogatory remarks about Liverpool Councillors, but that does not constitute an attack on the Party, and such things have happened often in the past.

We are told it is a group around a newspaper that some are out to get. I see from the press that the Labour Co-ordinating Committee is holding its Annual Meeting in Liverpool tomorrow, and the Secretary says it has 1,000 members nationally. Whether it is registered or not, the truth is surely that it is an organisation. What about Labour Solidarity, the heir to the Gang of Four, and all the other groups? Labour is a "Broad Church" and in my view should remain one.

The important thing to remember in this situation is that the Party has been here before. Various left-wingers in the Labour Party have been expelled in the past and action taken against Constituency Parties because they did not agree to go along with the actions of the NEC. The ironical fact is that some of those expelled either, when they were let back in, moved to the right, or are now referred to by most people in the Party as

Party stalwarts who were folk heroes, especially, of course, after they died.

The most prominent of the latter group is Aneurin Bevan. Today, we often hear Nye Bevan quoted and to some in high places in the Party he is a God-like figure. Yet he was one expelled, in 1938, from the Party, and almost expelled again after the Second World War when the Attlee Government had gone out of office.

The story of Nye Bevan's expulsion is told in Michael Foot's book about him. It is too long a story to be told in detail tonight, but it should be remembered. In 1932, the Socialist League was formed. According to Michael Foot, "The Socialist League mounted a big attack on what it regarded as the Party's unsevered attachment to 'gradualist' ideas." One of the leading figures was Stafford Cripps. Whilst at first Nye Bevan did not join the Socialist League, he did later because he felt Stafford Cripps was a cleaner and more wholesome influence on the Labour's leadership than any of the others. As Foot says, Bevan thought "Cripps' approach to Socialism might be crude, but was not a crude vitality greatly preferable to cynicism and lassitude?"

The basic cause of Bevan's expulsion was his support for Sir Stafford Cripps over the issue of the Popular Front. Whether one agrees or disagrees with the Popular Front concept, it was no reason to expel people from the Party. Cripps put forward a petition. He was expelled from the Party. Bevan said, "If every organised effort to change Party policy is to be described as an organised attack on the Party itself then the rigidity imposed by Party discipline will soon change into rigor mortis".

I would say to Party Leaders today, take note of what Nye Bevan then said, that the Party should take special care not to transform itself into "an intellectual concentration camp". He and George Strauss were given an ultimatum to withdraw from the Popular Front within seven days, or expulsion would follow automatically. There were others as well, some like Will Lawther and Sam Watson who complied with the NEC's edict.

The interesting point I want to make is that Nye Bevan, George Strauss, Cripps and others were actually defying party policy. Whilst their expulsions were totally wrong, the NEC could at least say they were out of tune with policy.

Here in Liverpool, the Party has been suspended and an investigation set up, not because the local Party has defied the

NEC and Party Conference, but because it has kept to Party policy, whilst others have not. The Liverpool Labour Group and Party have carried out the terms of the 1984 Conference decisions and on that they cannot be faulted. It is, therefore, disgraceful that the City Party should be suspended. I cannot recollect such a thing happening under Harold Wilson, Jim Callaghan or Michael Foot. It is reminiscent of the days of Gaitskell and Sarah Barker, when the right-wing totally dominated the Party, and when Ray Gunter was Chairman of the Organisation Committee — another one who finally left the Party and ended up by attacking socialist ideas.

After the Second World War, we were out of office for thirteen wasted years, 1951-1964. They were years when the left was under attack by the right — when Nye Bevan was again threatened with expulsion and was saved by one vote on the NEC, when the Bevanite Group was closed down, when Keep Left was outlawed, when there was a proscribed list, when tolerance was under severe pressure. I hope those days are not to return, and that the Party concentrates on fighting the Tory and Alliance enemy and not each other. That every effort is directed to winning the next election, so that we can begin to move towards a democratic socialist society.'

Tony Benn followed my contribution to the Liverpool meeting with a tremendous speech:

'No City and no people have suffered so much under capitalism as Liverpool. And never have I known such leadership in Liverpool as we have now. I'm proud to come here in support of the Councillors in their struggle to protect the people of the city against the Tories, and now alas against the attempts to suspend the District Labour Party.

From this platform I would like to appeal to the whole labour movement to support the Liverpool Councillors who are defending the people of this City from market forces and government cuts, and who — following conference policies — have prevented the massive rate rises and redundancies which the government hope to impose. Those councillors are threatened with surcharge, with bankruptcy, and with expulsion as well. I very much hope that constituency parties and trade unions throughout the country will support the Liverpool councillors and the Liverpool party, and support them with money and financial backing as they approach their appearance in court on 13 January.

I haven't come here to tell Liverpool how it should run its affairs. Over the last few years I've heard all our front-bench spokespeople saying in Parliament "don't interfere with local democracy". But when it comes to the internal affairs of the Party, I find the national executive taking a totally contrary view. There may have been mistakes made in Liverpool, I don't know. If so, I have made many myself. But any mistakes that are made in the labour movement are to be dealt with by discussion within the labour movement, in the area where the decisions are taken. They should not be used as an excuse for suspending the democracy of the Party.

Now let me turn to what is the strategy of the present NEC of the Labour Party — that has to be said too. It is a determined attempt to move to the centre, a shift of power to the Parliamentary Labour Party.

The Executive is being used not to produce policy like we had in Labour Programmes 1973, 1976 and 1982, but as a disciplinary force and to set conference decisions aside. Were those policies to be implemented we should have been sending a note of congratulation to the Liverpool Council. At the Bournemouth Conference, despite the media hype, a resolution was passed committing the party to compensate councillors who might be fined as a result of what they do.

What is at stake now is not the future of the Liverpool District Labour Party, but the future of the Labour Party itself, its historic role. To read the papers you'd think that Leon Trotsky (who I've read about, being a student of socialist history) when he was approaching the Winter Palace with a bayonet leading the Red Army, was not really worried about the Czar — he was planning the strategy of the Liverpool Council some 40 years after his death.

If you knock at a pensioner's house and say, "We're from the Labour Party. Are you keen on a better pension? Would you like a telephone? Would you like free fuel? Would you like a free bus service? Do you think perhaps we could hasten the hip operation you're waiting for?" They would say, "Yes, of course". But if you say you're Trotskyite, they shut the door and have a cup of Ovaltine to recover from the shock of what has been said to them.

The strategy which we have observed over the last two years has been designed to distance the Executive from those who have fought; distance them from the miners, from Liverpool, from our black community — distance them from the Left. The terrible danger is that by doing this, they confirm, by public attacks, the analysis of Tebbit and Thatcher. To turn on the radio and hear Norman Tebbit praising the National Executive of the Labour Party should tell us all we need to know about what is happening.

How should we respond? Not by sectarianism, because this is not a sectarian movement. Not by leaving the party, because it belongs to us. Not by splitting the party, because unity is strength. Not by personalising it, because our whole objection is that when they want to attack us they pick a personality and try to destroy that personality.

Our answer is to re-establish within the labour movement the traditions of socialism that brought it into being and gave it the greatest gains it had. Our business is to restate the demands that working people make: the right to work, the right to good education throughout life, the right to proper health care free at the point of need, the right to a good home, the right to dignity in retirement, the right to peace. That is our job: to restate those demands, and go on making them until they're met.

Our job is to rediscover solidarity, to rediscover internationalism. The struggle we are waging in Liverpool is exactly the same struggle as the miners, exactly the same struggle as the people of South Africa, exactly the same struggle as the people of Nicaragua and Turkey. The internationalism of capital, which would deny Liverpool the resources to earn a living, has got to be replaced by the internationalism of Labour.

We are going through very hard times at the moment. But having said all this, I believe the Labour and socialist Movement in Britain today is far stronger than at any time in my life. Stronger because of people like the Liverpool Councillors, the miners, and the black communities who stood up for their rights.

If we are a little bunch of loonie lefts, or whatever they call us, why does the media spend seven days a week, 52 weeks a year, trying to destroy us? Why is the Government giving the Police CS gas and riot weapons? It is because they know what we sometimes forget; that the ideas we advocate are stronger and more directly appealing to the British people than any which come from the City of London, the present Cabinet, the SDP or any other bunch of Tories.

What we are proving here in this City, and what I am proud

to come to say to you, is that if we stick by one another, if our objectives are honest and straightforward (as they are), if the courage and commitment is there, if our unity can be sustained — no power on earth can stop us from succeeding'.

In May 1986, the people of Liverpool gave their verdict on the Council's stand in the municipal elections. There had been gleeful predictions from some quarters of the movement that they would be heavily defeated. The reality turned out to be somewhat different. Labour lost only one seat and compensated for this by winning Breckfield in the Walton constituency. Dingle, the seat in which Labour was defeated, was lost by only 31 votes, less than the 44 votes received by the Communist Party candidate. In Speke Ward, Felicity Dowling, one of the twelve members faced with expulsion and ex-Secretary of the District Party, won with a majority of 1,800. The Conservative Party's vote virtually disappeared. In seats that had been considered rock solid for the Tories, the Alliance swept in with huge majorities.

On the day after the election David Hope, a journalist on the *Daily Post*, wrote 'Labour leader Neil Kinnock was left with a major headache last night after Liverpool rebels faced with bankruptcy and a High Court ban from office were given a storming vote of confidence by City electors. With the Party's NEC due shortly to consider expelling a dozen of their Militant colleagues, the solid support for three years of controversial policies must leave the Party with a puzzle'.

The victory was achieved in spite of a campaign of lies and slander from the Alliance. One of their leaflets was headed 'Gangsters run our town hall', a headline borrowed from the *Echo*. The leaflet quoted Roy Hattersley as saying on the 28th November 1985 'We know there has been political corruption. We know there has been literal corruption'.

Derek Hatton, as usual, was singled out for particular attack. It was claimed that his allowance from the Council amounted to £8,400 per year. John Hamilton and Hatton set the record straight in a leaflet they issued which pointed out that 75% of Hatton's allowance was repaid to his employer, Knowsley District Council, in compensation for the time taken off to attend to Council responsibilities.

John Hamilton summed up the results 'We've had a lot of problems this year with the courts and with our own Party nationally. But in the end people stood by us and our policies'.

The people of Liverpool, not for the first time, have shown a political maturity which is both remarkable and commendable. They have seen through the hostile lies about Liverpool's Labour Party from the media, the Tories, the Alliance and the Labour Party leadership. Roy Hattersley recently claimed on television in the north west that what Liverpool needed was a *'real* Labour Party'. In my opinion, Liverpool has got a *real* Labour Party, one which will fight with all its resources to ensure that the people of the City get a fairer deal and one that has returned me to Parliament for at least 21 years. The May 1986 elections demonstrate that the electorate of Liverpool accept this too. It is very sad that those in the leadership of the Party who are now prosecuting a witch hunt are not prepared to abide by the democratic will of party members and voters.

12
Groups Within the Party

Though the society in which we live still has broad class divisions it has also become increasingly fragmented. The Labour Party has experienced that fragmentation as much, if not more, than any other political organisation in Britain. In a sense it is a symptom of the break-up and crisis of capitalist society. Old patterns are changing, and so too is the working-class, for a variety of reasons.

In the prologue of his interesting book, *What Went Wrong?*, Jeremy Seabrook writes, 'Despite spectacular improvements there persists in working-class communities a malaise, an anger, a bitterness; ... clearly there is nothing wrong with material sufficiency; only the kind of materialism capital has achieved hurts ... We are robbed of our skills, and instead of being offered the opportunity to acquire new ones, we are invited to define ourselves by what we can buy rather than by what we can create'.

How true that is. The old skills, the old communities have been broken up. The sense of belonging, of being part of the group based on the workplace, has largely, though not entirely, disappeared. The old working-class is smaller than it was. However, it would be wrong to draw from this fact the conclusion that the Labour Party should no longer be based on the working class, or that socialist concepts are old-fashioned, and should be thrown out.

The Labour Party was, and still is, based on the organised

working-class. The fact that the majority of the members of trade unions have voted to retain the political levy, and with it affiliation to the Labour Party, is evidence of that. Certainly the composition of this working class is different. In the Party today, there are more white collar workers: university lecturers, school teachers, social workers, Local Government employees and so on. Many are the sons and daughters of workers who, because of the educational policies of past Labour Governments in particular, had the opportunity of going to University and getting a higher education denied to most working class people prior to the end of the Second World War.

A lot of these students were at college during the days of the Wilson Governments of 1964/70 and were active in the student upsurge of 1968. They were very much involved in the campaign against the Vietnam war, and were disillusioned with the Wilson Government which supported that war. Many of them joined small political groups, mainly of a Marxist hue, like the International Socialists, the Socialist Labour League, the International Marxist Group, and a host of others. They were young socialists, who should have been part of the Labour Party, but were not, because they disagreed with Wilson's policies on a range of issues.

I have long held the view that all socialists should be part of the Labour Party. It is a view based on personal experience. I first joined the Labour Party when I was about 16 or 17 years of age but soon became disenchanted with it because I felt it was not bold enough in the fight against fascism, and was not socialist enough. Consequently I joined the Communist Party and remained a member until 1948 when I was expelled for being a 'left-wing deviationist' along with a group of friends in the Welwyn Garden City Party. Raph Samuel refers to this group in a recent issue of *New Left Review* and is mistaken when he writes that the 'Welwyn comrades ... took up a position rather similar to that later adopted by the Party itself'. The Party did change its policy towards a more class-orientated position later, but we in the Welwyn Garden City and Hertford and Ware Branches, felt that the Party was repudiating its Leninist revolutionary position and was becoming totally reformist in character. We objected, for example, to the idea of a Government of national unity at the end of the war, including progressive Tories like Churchill and Eden, and felt the Party should have supported from the outset the election of a Labour

Government. We also objected to the Party being opposed to strikes and calling for all-out production. Theoretically, we supported Lenin's ideas and argued against the leadership from a Leninist position. The Revolutionary Communist Party (RCP) at the time thought we might be won to them, but we were not Trotskyists, and I am afraid remained, to some extent, Stalinists for quite a long time, even after we had been expelled.

Because I would not join any of the Trotskyist groups, I rejoined the Labour Party in 1948. I must say I was surprised to find that Trotskyists who had tried to recruit me earlier were now in the Labour Party. But as the RCP had folded up I saw nothing wrong with that. No doubt they were, or some of them, following the entry tactic advanced by Trotsky to the French Trotskyists in the 1930s, but all that mattered to me was that they were real socialists, fighting for socialist policies.

Over the course of the next few years I became increasingly impatient at the way the Labour Party was going. I remained unattracted to the Communist Party, but felt the Labour Party was too right-wing. Together with Harry McShane, Walter Kendall and others, I tried to form the basis of a new party which would be a type of Independent Labour Party with a more positive revolutionary outlook and left the Labour Party as an individual member in 1954. At that time, on behalf of the group known as the Socialist Workers Federation (SWF), I approached other groups, some in the Labour Party, to see if they would discuss with us the creation of a new party. We got nowhere and, when we realised we were outside the main stream of the workers' movement, we disbanded. Some, like Harry McShane, never joined any other Party, whilst others like myself re-joined the Labour Party. I had a little difficulty in re-joining but was eventually allowed into the Toxteth Party. Quite soon afterwards I was elected Chairman. During my time with the SWF, I remained a delegate to the Liverpool Trades Council and Labour Party (being eligible because I was paying the political levy and was not a member of a proscribed organisation).

I give this background so that my attitude to the various groups and movements inside the Labour Party can be understood. Since my personal experience of being on the fringes of the movement, I have always believed that all socialists should be in the Labour Party. If some are in groups formed around newspapers, they should as individuals support their papers and fight for their ideas. They should compete with others to get the ear of the Party. Some years ago, I wrote an article for the *New Statesman* outlining these ideas. I also urged, when the Party issued its pamphlet on Eurocommunism, that the Communist Party should disband and its members join the Labour Party, whilst at the same time keeping their paper, the *Morning Star*, if they wished. Some in the CP were very angry with me at the time and this anger spilled over in the paper. I cannot agree to people being expelled because they are organised around newspapers.

In Liverpool there have been Militant supporters for a very long time. In recent years they have become more prominent because they filled a gap left by others on the Left. They clearly accept many of Trotsky's ideas but, like the CP, they have evolved from the positions which the original Bolsheviks stood for. They are now deeply rooted in the Labour Party and to that extent are as much a part of the political debate inside the organization as the Bevanites and other groups such as the Socialist League of Stafford Cripps were in the past. This is not to say that I accept or agree with all of Militant's arguments and policies for I do not. But the way to deal with all arguments is to beat them in discussion, by putting forward better positions and developing support for them. Only in this way can we ensure that the Party remains a genuine broad church with a mass membership, taking in all sections of the working-class and the population.

I always thought the Marxist Social Democratic Federation were sectarian in leaving the Labour Party as they did so soon after it was formed. Had they not left it, the Party may well have been a very different one. The ILP were also wrong to leave the Party in 1932, a move which lost the Left a great deal of influence. The ILP was in a difficult position at the time, and it was well nigh impossible for them to accept the conditions the Party leadership had laid down, but looking back, despite all the provocation, it was obviously a great mistake for them to have left.

At the moment, there are a number of papers and groups competing with each other for the ear of the Party. They range from the far left to the far right in Party terms and that is how it should be. Whilst, as a dedicated left winger, I want to see the views in which I believe prevail, nevertheless I believe that anyone who accepts the constitution and programme of the Party has a right to be a member and advocate within it their own particular ideas of socialism.

In any case, internal groupings are not only restricted to the rank and file of the Party. There are currently three groups organized within the Parliamentary Party, the Solidarity Group on the right, the Campaign Group on the left, and the Tribune Group which now occupies a centre left position. The latter was formed after Labour's victory in 1964 and was the heir to the old Bevan group which had been forced to disband. I was a founding member along with Ian Mikardo, Stan Orme, Norman Atkinson and Norman Buchan. The group then could call on a remarkable array of talent including Sydney Silverman, Konni Zilliacus, Emrys Hughes, Michael Foot, Harold Davies, William Warby and many others.

Today, the Tribune Group is a shadow of its former self. Although it still includes many excellent left-wingers it has increasingly become a vehicle for those in search of Ministerial office at the expense of its role as an organization fighting for left policies within the PLP. The fact that Tribune officers recently rushed to attack the seven NEC members who walked out of the National Executive meeting called to expel Liverpool Militants without even consulting members of the group is indicative of the decline in Tribune. But despite this rightward shift, I was opposed to the decision by Tony Benn, Dennis Skinner, Joan Maynard and others to split from Tribune in order to set up the Campaign Group and I remain so today. Had the left stayed within Tribune it would not have been so easy for the right to influence it in the way they have. Nevertheless, I was forced to accept the reality of what had happened and after Tribune condoned the investigation of the Liverpool Party I had no choice but to leave it, with a heavy heart, after 21 years membership.

The Campaign Group, of which I am now a member, has taken up the banner that Tribune allowed to fall. It played an important role in solidarising with the miners whilst they were on strike and, through the good work of Dennis Skinner and Brian Sedgemore, has tenaciously exposed the machinations of the City of London. It was also a Campaign Group member, Tam Dalyell, who with considerable persistence, exposed Mrs Thatcher's notorious role in the General Belgrano affair.

The group is encouraging the formation of Campaign Groups in cities and towns throughout Britain thereby attempting to combine Parliamentary and extra-Parliamentary activity.

It is also attempting to maintain and deepen its links with the trade union movement and it is to be hoped that Campaign meetings will become a regular feature of trade union conferences. If I have any criticism of the Group at all it is that it could play a more active role in Parliament, as the old Tribune Group did, with more Early Day Motions, more Parliamentary questions, and more initiatives like the one where its members stood in front of the Mace in an attempt to stop the proceedings of the House of Commons in order to draw attention to the plight of miners' families during the NUM strike.

The Solidarity Group is probably the strongest organization within the Parliamentary Party and certainly should not be underestimated. They have a successful record in getting people elected to the Shadow Cabinet. In the last elections the joint Campaign Group/Tribune list ensured the election of five candidates. The remaining ten winners came either from the Solidarity Group or were supported by it. They consequently have a 2 to 1 majority in the Shadow Cabinet.

The politics of the Solidarity Group do not sometimes seem very different from those who left the Party to form the SDP though, of course, they are dressed up in the language of socialism. On the 13th November 1984, for instance, the *Times* reported that 'The centre-right Labour Solidarity Group ... issued a strong statement yesterday, warning Labour-controlled councils to stay within the law over the Government's expenditure restraints ... The statement rejects a conference decision to support law-breaking councils and reflects a new aggressive response to the left's advances'.

The Solidarity Group is currently on the offensive. Stuart Bell, the Secretary of the group who entered Parliament in 1983, told the *Guardian* recently 'We are cranking up our organization. We feel confident that the Labour Party is swinging back to traditional values and the Freedom and Fairness campaign is an indication of that. We feel we should come out of the Parliamentary bunker'. Despite the fighting talk, it is my belief that Solidarity recognises it cannot win outright within the Party as a whole and sees its best way forward through marginalising the Campaign Group by striking agreements with some of the soft left whilst at the same time directing the Party rightwards through the Parliamentary Party.

If such groups as Solidarity, Tribune and the Campaign Group operate freely inside the Party, the question must surely be asked, why is it that other groups, openly committed to socialist ideas, are being harrassed and expelled? I believe the witch-hunt which is currently underway is unjust and arbitrary. It is important to make clear the basis on which individuals and groups are liable to exclusion from the Party. This should only be if they i) stand candidates against the Party, ii) refuse to accept the constitution and programme of the Party, and iii) if they are individually intending to disrupt the Party, as has been the case with some individuals in recent years. Before expulsion takes place there must be a scrupulously fair system of appeal. It has been suggested that the Party might consider electing an appeals body, separate from the NEC — a suggestion which I believe requires further consideration.

It is frequently suggested that groups within Labour's ranks constitute separate parties within the Party. There is undeniably a grain of truth in this. Any organisation within the Party must to some extent have a membership with a dual loyalty, a commitment to both the Labour Party itself and to the organization that is working for its objectives within it. There is nothing wrong with that provided the group takes the view that its objectives are to maintain, protect and develop the fundamental principles of the Party. We have always been a federal organization and should not fear changing back towards a more federal, decentralised structure.

The Labour Party has never been a democratic centralist organization and in my view should never become one. Democratic centralism is advocated by both the Communist Party and the Trotskyist groups. It is a theory which allows democratic discussion within the organization but demands that all members present the majority position in public. In practice the centralist half of the equation has tended to dominate the democratic half.

The argument about the role of centralism within socialist parties goes back to the split between the Mensheviks and Bolsheviks at the Second Congress of the Russian Social Democratic Party. Lenin had drafted a resolution on membership for the Congress which stated 'A member of the Party is any person who accepts its programme, supports the Party with material means, and personally participates in one of its organisations'. Martov, with the support of Trotsky, proposed that 'personally participates' be replaced by 'co-operate personally and regularly under the guidance of one of the organisations'. It may seem a minor difference, but it indicated that Lenin wanted a tighter organisation and Martov a much looser one. Martov was prepared to drop his draft as he felt it unnecessary to split over such a paragraph. However, the differences in emphasis became magnified and the issue became the central focus of the debate. Instead of emerging as one party, the party divided into two.

Trotsky, outside the Bolshevik Party, developed his differences with Lenin in articles and pamphlets. He described Lenin's position as a call for 'orthodox theory' which would 'substitute itself for the working classes' and would act as a proxy in the name of what the workers felt or thought: 'The party organisation (ie. the caucus) at first substitutes itself for the party as a whole; the Central Committee substitutes itself for the organisation; and finally a single "dictator" substitutes himself for the Central Committee ...'. Trotsky argued 'The Party must seek the guarantee of its stability in its own bases, in an active proletariat and not in a top caucus ...' and pointed out that 'A Jacobin tribunal would have tried under the charge of moderation the whole international Labour Movement, and Marx's lion head would have been the first to roll under the guillotine'. He ended his argument by stating 'The tasks of the new regime will be so complex that they cannot be solved otherwise than by way of a competition between various methods of economic and political construction, by way of long "disputes", by way of a systematic struggle not only between the socialist and the capitalist worlds, but also between many trends inside socialism, trends which will inevitably emerge as soon as the proletarian dictatorship poses tens and hundreds of new problems ... A proletariat capable of exercising its dictatorship over society will not tolerate any dictatorship over itself. The working class ... will undoubtedly have in its ranks quite a few political invalids ... and much ballast of obsolescent ideas, which it will have to jettison.... But the intricate task cannot be solved by placing above the proletariat a few well picked people ... or one person invested with the power to liquidate and degrade'.

It was a powerful attack on Lenin's ideas, and on Lenin himself, and whilst in part unfair (Lenin had not expelled a single member from the Party), I believe Trotsky's point about basic organisation was absolutely correct. Later, after the 1917 revolution, Trotsky joined the Bolshevik Party and completely accepted the Leninist concept of party organisation. He suffered greatly for it after Stalin had won control of the party and went on to carry out precisely what the younger Trotsky had warned could happen.

It is useful, in this context, to consider also the views of that great revolutionary Rosa Luxemburg. She gave her unqualified support to the Russian revolution and to the Bolsheviks. When the revolution first took place, before the October revolution, she wrote, 'The revolution in Russia has been victorious over Absolutism at the first onset but this victory is not the end of the struggle; it is only the beginning'.

Luxemburg's first reaction to the Bolshevik revolution was recorded in a letter to Louise Kautsky. She fully supported what had happened but was worried about the revolution's future '... because Social Democracy in the highly developed West is represented by a pack of pitiful cowards who are prepared to look on inactively whilst the Russians shed their hearts' blood'. She made her position clear in a small book, *The Russian Revolution*. She was critical of the way things were developing in the Soviet Union and said so in the strongest terms. She was totally opposed to freedom of criticism being suppressed, whether that criticism was from friends or enemies of the Soviet regime. She considered that such dissent was the only real guarantee against the bureaucratic degeneration of the new state apparatus. She argued that constant public control, freedom of the press and complete freedom of assembly was necessary. She put it this way:

'Freedom for supporters of the Government only, for the members of one pary only — no matter how big its membership may be — is no freedom at all. Freedom is always freedom for the men who think differently. This contention does not spring from a fanatical love of abstract "Justice"; but from the fact that everything which is healthy and purifying in political freedom derives from its independent character and from the fact that freedom loses all its virtue when it becomes a privilege ... The suppression of political life throughout the country must gradually cause the vitality of the Soviets themselves to decline. Without general elections, freedom of the press, freedom of assembly, and freedom of speech, life in every public institution slows down, becomes a caricature of itself, and bureaucracy rises as the only deciding factor. No one can escape the workings of this law. Public life gradually dies, and a few dozen party leaders with inexhaustible energy and limitless idealism direct and rule ... In the last resort cliquism develops a dictatorship, but not dictatorship of the proletariat; the dictatorship of a handful of politicians, i.e. a dictatorship in the bourgeois sense, in the Jacobin sense ...'

The practice of, and debate around, centralism has continued to the present day. It has contributed significantly in recent times to splits in the Communist Party and the Workers Revolutionary Party. It has also figured largely in debates within the Labour Party on the issue of democracy. In his book, *For a Pluralist Socialism*,[1] Michael Rustin examines the relationship of the New Left of the 1950s with the Labour Party. He writes 'If the radical intelligentsia of the New Left has found itself devoid of a firm political foothold for most of its history, the main alternative site of socialist activity, the Labour Party, has been no success story either and goes on 'There is no future for the Labour Party in attempting to reconstitute a trade union and parliamentary duopoly. To this extent the constitutional reforms of 1980 which attempted to confer greater powers on the mass party membership were justified and necessary'.

This is a view I hold. I believe the party needs to build up its workplace branches, women's sections, affiliated Black, Asian and ethnic sections, and accept that as there must be a pluralist socialism in today's world, there must be a pluralist Labour Party with room for different trends, tendencies and ideas, providing they are united around the basic socialist tenets of the Party.

Whilst democratic centralism must be rejected, we should be careful not to let a dismissal of a particular form of political organization become confused with the Marxist framework within which it has operated. Marxism certainly has a place in today's Labour Party and has always made a great contribution to Labour's ideas. One of the best of the little books about Marxism, *What is Marxism?* was written by A.L. Williams (Len Williams), for the National Council for Labour Colleges. J.P.M. Miller, General Secretary of the NCLC, wrote in the introduction, 'It is the purpose of this pamphlet to explain in a short and simple fashion who Marx was and what Marxism is. The man who does not understand Marxism is only half-educated. The man who does has in his possession one of the

1. *For a Pluralist Socialism* by Michael Rustin. Verso 1985.

greatest intellectual tools ever forged by the human mind'. I was part of a group which tried to get this publication circulated by the Labour Party but the NEC would not agree to it.

Today, compared with the days of my youth, the books by Marx and about Marxism are more widely available and more numerous. But whilst there are university courses in this field there has been little education, since the collapse of the NCLC, amongst working class organisations in the basics of Marxism. The various Marxist groups have helped fill the gap left by the NCLC. *Socialist Action, Socialist Organiser, Militant, The Morning Star, Labour Leader* and many others, do an important job of helping to teach young workers the nature of society, the character of the State, and the centrality of class struggle. It would be a serious retrograde step if such papers were banned for sale in the Party, and their supporters driven out.

The Labour Party has never been a uniform body, though some in the leadership who have opposed democratic centralism in theory have come close to carrying it out in practice. There are other movements, apart from the Marxists, in the broader socialist body which have great merit. One example is the Christian Socialist Movement which has just published *Facing the Future as Christians and Socialists*, marking the 25th anniversary of its existence. In the introduction, Herbert McCabe is quoted as saying, 'The daily news from Latin America shows Christians as posing a far greater threat to business interests than communist parties ever did'. For too long, the Church of England has been regarded as the Tory Party at prayer. Yet the Church has always had a radical trend within it. It was the Reverend Charles Kingsley, an early Christian Socialist in the last century, who said, 'I am a Church of England clergyman, and I am a Chartist'. It is important to recall that in the Anglican Communion, there have always been such outstanding socialist figures as F.D. Maurice, Stewart Hedlam, Conrad Noel and John Groser. Today there is the Jubilee Group. If the policy of proscription were to be re-introduced in the Labour Party, then membership of such a body as the Christian Socialists could conceivably be outlawed.

Another organisation which is open to both Labour Party and non-Labour Party members is the Socialist Society. This could be described as a left-wing Fabian Society, something I have long thought the movement needed. Since the NCLC went out of existence, the Workers' Control Movement with Spokesman

Books, has done a good job in educating and organising debate. But clearly something more is needed, and the Socialist Society could be the organisation to fill the gap. It may well, however, produce pamphlets and hold meetings which are extremely critical of the official Party line. Should we then say that Party members could not join the Society? Of course not; the Labour Party must allow pluralism amongst its own membership, as well as supporting pluralism in the wider political sense.

The days of the proscriptions were not good days. They kept good people out of the Party and I hope they do not return. That is why I have always been against the internal Register of Groups. If groups wish to become registered that is a matter for them, but it is wrong that those who decide not to register should be discriminated against.

The Labour Party prides itself on not being democratic centralist. What worries me today, however, is that it is getting more centralist and less democratic. There are those who argue that the existence of groups within the Party is fissiparous. A similar argument was used against groups in the Bolshevik Party. In that organisation they were disbanded with ultimately dire results. I do not deny that life might be easier without internal groupings but it is good for democracy, and in my view, important for discussion and debate within the Party.

I would like to see frank and open discussion of all issues involving individuals and anyone who supports a particular newspaper or belongs to a group within the Party. Such discussions, properly channelled, can only help to mobilise the Party to work in a united way to defeat this Government. The alternative is ever greater central control, and if that happens, then enthusiasm will wane, initiative will cease and the Party will become merely a centralised machine geared only to winning elections. Under these circumstances it is unlikely to be successful in such endeavour.

13
Labour at the Crossroads

The Labour Party's path has never been smooth and easy. Since its formation it has known great achievements and miserable failures. Its highest achievement was when it received the biggest vote ever recorded in Britain for a political party in the 1951 General Election. It nonetheless lost that election because of Parliamentary boundary changes. The people wanted Labour, but got instead a Conservative government which bene-fitted from what Labour had achieved during its six previous years in office. Following their defeat, as could be expected, an inquest took place within the Party. The right-wing put the blame for defeat on the left who, it argued, had caused prob-lems by not supporting the Government's policy on National Health Service prescription charges (Nye Bevan had resigned on this issue), not always supporting the Government's foreign policy, and by criticizing the Morrisonian policy of 'consolida-tion'. The right felt the Party should drop the more socialist clauses of the Constitution — Clause IV was singled out for attack.

The struggle that developed after the 1951 defeat was between those who wished to retain the party's socialist base, to develop and extend it, and those who wanted to change the Party into a type of European Social Democratic Party, or even worse, a sort of US Democratic Party. The trade unions, being working class in character despite having right-wing leaders, insisted on keeping Clause IV. It was a time of real upheaval in the Labour Party. Some people at local level were expelled and, at one stage, Bevan himself was threatened with expulsion. In the PLP Labour MPs on the different sides of the divide did not speak to one another, the PLP divided into two warring camps. Today, that is not the situation in the PLP and I trust it will not become so. However, the danger of such a development is a real one.

During the Gaitskell period left-wing MPs were suspended from the PLP and had the whip withdrawn because they voted against or abstained on votes concerning Tory Government defence expenditure. Michael Foot, Emrys Hughes, Sydney Silverman and others were amongst the victims and were still outside the PLP when Harold Wilson was elected as Leader. Harold Wilson was elected to bring the Party together. In *Harold Wilson — a Pictorial Biography*,[1] Michael Foot wrote 'His instinctive responses to a situation are likely to be those of rank and file members of the party. For all his sophisticated abilities, he is not at loggerheads or out of sympathy with those he aspires to lead. His intellectual kinship with them has deep roots'.

It can be argued that in later years Wilson was not always in tune with the grass roots, and did find himself in conflict with party members. But before the 1964 General Election there was little antagonism between Wilson and the rank and file, and when there was, he did not resort to harsh administrative measures against them. The worst disciplining in the PLP after Wilson became Prime Minister was the banning of some of us from PLP meetings for a short period. Frankly this did not seem such a terrible hardship. It was Wilson, together with John Silkin, who 'liberalised' the Standing Orders of the PLP.

Party conflict undoubtedly diminished when Harold Wilson took over. He was never a real left-wing socialist, but he was left of centre and had resigned from the Government with Nye Bevan and John Freeman at one stage of the Party's history. He kept the Party together in his first years as Leader, with the left-wing giving him support in the early days and even at critical times later when it was clear that he was having trouble with the right. The Party's fortunes began to be restored without Wilson

---

1. *Harold Wilson — A Pictorial Biography* by Michael Foot. Pergamon Press, 1964.

pandering to the Tory press and attacking his own left-wing.

Michael Foot also states that it was a failure on the part of Wilson's opponents to understand his rapport with grass root members which led them to give false explanations of his popularity amongst his followers. They asked 'What sinister magic has enabled him to inspire such unaccustomed unity in his Party? Why has he not staged stubborn battles with obstreperous followers? — always a valued trait in left-wing leaders among Tories'. Wilson has often quoted Nye Bevan's speech of the 1959 Labour Party Conference part of which said, 'Parliamentary institutions have not been destroyed because the left is too vigorous; they have been destroyed because they were too inert; we have never suffered from too much audacity; we have suffered from too little'. Unfortunately, when Wilson came to office, audacity to attack capitalism rapidly waned and there were further upheavals inside the Party over the Prices and Incomes policy, 'In Place of Strife', the Vietnam War, the seamen's strike and a host of other issues.

Since 1951, the Labour Party's share of the votes has declined. It is important that the Party closely examines why and where this has happened. Why, for example, did Liverpool and other parts of the country retain and win the support of the voters, whilst in other working class areas support fell away? It would have been better if such an analysis had been developed by the Party organisation after the 1983 defeat, before it rushed into an election for a new Leader with a very superficial analysis of the election results.

After every electoral defeat since 1951 there have been groups and individuals in the Party who have wanted it to drop the basic socialist policies which, they argued, have been responsible for its defeat. In 1956, a group calling itself 'Socialist Union', published a book *Twentieth Century Socialism*.[2] Prominent members of the group were Rita Hinden and Allen Flanders. Theirs was a revisionist position rather than a total rejection of Socialism, but their book paved the way for the great debate in which Hugh Gaitskell attempted to change the Party Constitution and policy by getting rid of Clause IV. In *Twentieth Century Socialism*, the question of common owner-

---

2. *Twentieth Century Socialism* by Socialist Union. Penguin Books, 1956.

ship is discussed: 'The case for complete common ownership rested on a number of mistaken concepts. The first of these was the belief that the private ownership of capital was a bad thing in itself. One side of the coin of private ownership is undoubtedly power which can be abused. Yet looking at the coin from the other side, private ownership can also be seen as a condition of freedom'.

As in most matters, there was some truth in what the revisionists said. They rightly pointed out, for example, that abuse could take place under public as well as private ownership, something which has been proved beyond doubt in the Soviet Union and other Eastern European countries. What they argued for in 1956 was to some extent, in a very different context, what Labour actually came up with in 1974, in its proposals for the formation of the NEB. The right, at that stage, were not prepared to make a total frontal attack on the basic concepts of the Party, but it was obvious that a dilution of socialist policy was underway and, soon afterwards, the NEC of the Party produced a thoroughly revisionist document, *Industry and Society* which was opposed at Party Conference by MPs like Maurice Edelman, and Willie Ross.

It was not until after the defeat of the Wilson/Callaghan Government in 1979 that the Party began moving steadily to the left. The right wing continued to be strong in the PLP, but the NEC, and with it Party policy, moved towards clearer socialist positions. The Manifesto of 1979 was one of the most left-wing since 1945. In the face of an advancing left some of the right decided to work and prepare for a split in the Party. After their departure in 1981, many felt that from now on the Party would keep to a sound, socialist path. But it was not to be: the defeat of the Party at the 1983 election led to a recovery of the right which speeded up after Neil Kinnock's election. At the 1983 NEC following the Conference, left-wing Chairmen like Tony Benn and myself were replaced in office by people more to the right. Now only two left-wingers have retained their Chairs on the NEC, David Blunkett and Tom Sawyer, and both have recently supported views that indicate a shift in their political positions.

I believe that the Party today has to take a tremendously important decision as to the direction in which it is going. Is it to remain a basically socialist party, or is it to become a sort of Social Democratic Party Mark 2? The signs are that it is moving in the latter direction. For a short period after the leadership election the direction the party was taking was not clear. The election of the 'Dream Ticket' was supposed to be a balance between right and left and this confused many people. But very quickly, at higher levels if not at grass-roots, the Party was tilted to the right. Some on the left began to talk about the Leader being captured by the right, that Neil Kinnock was a prisoner who needed saving from those on the Shadow Cabinet around him. All of this was very interesting at the time, but in the light of subsequent events it was irrelevant. The membership has now clearly been told that the Party is moving in a new direction. It could, of course, be moving sideways, upwards, or downwards, retaining the same political positions but pushing for them in a different way. But it is not; the move is rapidly right-wards.

The future of the Party is now a matter of intense public debate. Anthony Barnett, for example, wrote an article for *New Socialist*, which raised the posibility of a future coalition government with the SDP. Neil Kinnock replied to Barnett's piece by describing it as 'bilious'. His opposition to any idea of coalitions and PR can only be welcomed. Barnett, however, is on stronger ground when he argues that Britain is in a situation where old answers to problems are no longer applicable. Welfare capitalism is failing fast, Keynesian policies will no longer suffice. To get back to full employment requires socialist planning, public ownership and positive Government intervention in economic and industrial affairs. That is why the Labour Party must offer a real ideological option. If it fails to do so then there is no reason why voters should not turn to the 'new' option of the SDP. A Labour Party that is in essence an SDP Mark 2 has no real future unless it either merges with the SDP or splits and a genuinely socialist party is formed.

There is some force in the argument that if you change direction, as the Party has, then a compromise with like-minded political forces is bound to be the logical conclusion. That is at the core of Barnett's argument. If the Party is going along the path of repudiating the left, revising its policies, turning rightwards, then why not seek an agreement with the SDP/Liberal Alliance? As the *Guardian* editorial of 6th January 1986 put it, 'This Government is highly unpopular. Most of the country doesn't like it. But how do you turn that antipathetic majority into a force that sends Prime Minister Kinnock to Downing Street? By proclaiming a desirable world, what ever the facts of the matter?

Or by addressing the new situation that you yourself, by your campaign against the hard left and your reversings of policy have helped in part to create'.

Support for a political strategy of winning the Alliance to a broad popular front opposing Thatcherism comes from another source: the Eurocommunists of the British Communist Party and in particular, their intellectual guru, the distinguished historian Eric Hobsbawm. Without ever actually calling for a formal alliance between Labour and the SDP and Liberals, Hobsbawm has consistently advocated that the Party should be prepared to co-operate with the Alliance in order to keep Thatcher out.

The position advanced by Hobsbawm and other Euro-communists like Bob Rowthorn and Dave Prescott is, in essence, a revision to the type of argument for a government of 'national unity' put forward by the Communist Party towards the end of the Second World War when the party leadership argued that such a government should include 'progressive' Tories like Churchill and Eden. It also draws heavily on the politics and experience of the Italian Communist Party, the PCI, whose search for a 'historic compromise' with sections of the Italian ruling class has been a governing strategic objective. I have the greatest admiration for the PCI. It is a genuine mass party of the Italian working class. But to translate the situation they face in Italy directly into a British context is a major mistake. It ignores the vital asset which Hobsbawm admits Labour has: 'The capacity to win an election and form a government single-handed'. It is that asset which caused Labour in the late 1930s to reject the Popular Front, and which made Labour go all out for Government in 1945 instead of the 'national unity' administration advocated by the CP. That asset must today be the cornerstone of Labour's forward thinking.

It is the pessimism of Eurocommunists like Eric Hobsbawm which I find most depressing. For them, the struggle for socialism must be postponed. Their constant theme is that the central task facing the workers movement is the removal of Thatcher. What replaces her is of secondary importance. I argued against this view as far back as 1975 when in an article 'Two Labour Parties or One?' for the *Political Quarterly*, I wrote 'The left view is that the crisis of capitalism must be the occasion to introduce socialist measures and move towards a classless, egalitarian society. This is the very opposite of those who say "Get the crisis over first, then move towards socialism later". The fact is that once the immediate crisis is over and the pressure is off, then the opportunities for getting measures through which can lead towards socialism are lost and it becomes more difficult at a later stage'.

Hobsbawm's views on the prospects for socialism are founded on a belief that class politics are no longer key in the struggle. Whilst he has highlighted important changes in the structure of the working class in recent years which need to be taken into account in Labour's campaigns and policies, I believe he and the other Eurocommunists are quite mistaken in emphasising what they see as a fall in the importance of the workers movement. Labour must certainly bring its propaganda and methods up to date by taking into account the shift from manual to white collar and service jobs within the working class. It must not, however, abandon its basic class orientation. If it does, the core of its base of support will disappear and it will be little different from other reformist capitalist parties.

Hobsbawm's analysis leads him to delight in attacking the left of the Labour Party. In the April 1985 issue of *Marxism Today*, for instance, he writes that 'Labour remains the mass force of opposition, and is likely to remain so unless the sectarians have their way and reduce it to yet another rump sect, which is — luckily — no longer very probable'. Such attacks have encouraged some in the leadership of the Party to adopt Hobsbawm's revisionism as a theoretical justification for their own drift to the right. It is in this respect that the Euro-communists pose a real threat to Labour. Organizationally, the British Communist Party is extremely weak. Recent splits have seen the membership of the Party falling towards the 10,000 mark. Politically bankrupt and irrelevant in their own right, the arguments they are advancing for a popular front only become dangerous when they are taken up by those with positions of real influence inside the Party. Because this *is* happening, it is important that socialists take issue with the Eurocommunists to reassert Labour's role as a socialist Party, based on the working class, and fighting for government on its own terms and not those dictated by the need to strike alliances with parties and currents whose policies in power would differ little from those Thatcher has been pursuing for the past seven years.

Up to now, the 1982 Party Programme has not been repudiated, although the policies have been attacked by a number of leading people in the Party. I believe there will not be a frontal attack on the Programme. It is much more likely to be bypassed and ignored, with new policies or old Gaitskellite policies restored by stealth. In fighting to prevent these we lay ourselves open to critics who will say that we are living in the past. They will refer us to what Keir Hardie wrote about in 1904, in the *Labour Leader*, 'A great principle may be so overlain by dogmatic interpretation as to be unrecognisable; nay, the dogma may in course of time come to be considered of greater importance than the principle itself. It is well, therefore, to examine all formulas and phrases which we are told are not only part and parcel of the true doctrine, but the only real interpretation thereof'. This is a substantial point, and one that cannot be ignored or brushed aside. But it is not, the exact wording, the phraseology, that I am concerned about, it is the principle. One does not have to be tied to a particular formula forever. It is important, at times, that we modernise our language, and thrust aside dogmatic approaches. However we must retain our basic socialist objectives and it is these which are now under threat.

There are two ways of dropping Labour's socialism. There is the Gaitskell way, open and honest like the man himself, and there is the other way, killing it off by kindness, paying lip service to it but in reality ignoring it. That, I fear, is the danger today, and in this connection, I stand by what I myself wrote in the *Labour Leader* in October 1985: 'I am deeply concerned at some of the ideas that are being floated and pursued in the movement. We are witnessing a wholesale revisionism of socialist ideas, the abandonment of genuine socialist revolutionary politics and an attempt by some to turn the Labour Party into another SDP. This process has been helped by some on the so-called Left, who only a few years ago were fanatical supporters of Tony Benn, when he stood for the Deputy Leadership. Some have become arch revisionists. This is unforgiveable because such positions neither give us an electoral victory short term or fundamental social changes long term ... The Party faces two dangers. First a revisionist, reformist drift to the right, and secondly a response to that drift which is sectarian. The former problem at the moment is greater than the latter. If we have policies which are indistinguishable from those of the Social Democrats, it will not be Labour that benefits, but our enemies. It will be the road to defeat. Clarifying, updating, even changing certain policies is perfectly acceptable, providing they rest on basic socialist foundations. After six years of Thatcherism, a socialist programme is more important than ever'.

Fashionable political commentators are once again declaring that socialism is dead. Brian Walden, who writes in the *London Standard*, is a leading exponent of this theory. According to Walden, 'Socialism as understood by its impassioned followers cannot now be brought about in Britain ... Certainly, you won't see the abolition of private ownership and "production for use not profit"'. The reason, he argues, is that the working class don't want this, and to get the workers' votes, Labour must water down its doctrine to 'the point where one can hardly taste the essence. If not the workers won't touch it'. This is why, he says, 'all Labour Governments in Britain "betray" socialism. It is written all over Mr Kinnock — a sensible and realistic chap — that if he ever formed a government, he would be one of the greatest "betrayers" of socialism'.

In Walden's view, the Labour Party does not need socialism. It can win much more easily without it: 'Socialism is the cuckoo that laid its egg in Labour's promising nest. Its offspring drove everything else out'. Gaitskell, he points out, tried to flush the socialist illusions down the tubes and failed; but the opportunity to do so has arrived again. It is undoubtedly true that Gaitskell did weaken Labour's socialist resolve and this was clearly understood by the Party membership and Labour supporters. But Labour did not come near to winning an election under his leadership. It was Wilson, who at least continued to partially talk the language of socialism (even though it was not the socialism of the left), who won in 1964, and who did so by uniting the Party around the policies which included public ownership and other socialist proposals.

In effect what Walden is saying is that Labour can only win elections if it becomes an SDP Mark 2 and abandons any pretence of socialist policies. Like many others before him, he has too early and too easily described the death of socialism. He long ago gave up the socialist cause, when he left the Labour Party and took up a T.V. presenter's job with London Weekend Television. Even before then he refused a Minister's job in the Labour Government because he said it would not pay him enough money. He is mistaken, too, about the birth of socialism in the Labour Party.

When the Party was formed in 1900 it did not, it is true, have socialism as an objective and it was not until 1918 that socialism was written into the constitution. It was, however, allowed to join the Socialist Second International in 1906. At the time, Karl Kautsky, the leading German Social-Democrat, explained that, 'The English Labour Party is to be admitted to the International Socialist Congress because although it does not avowedly recognise the class struggle, it actually carries it on; and because the organisation of the Labour Party being independent of the bourgeois parties is based on the class struggle'.

Socialism was not a cuckoo in Labour's nest. The Party accepted socialism in its constitution because it recognised that it could not deal with the problems of unemployment and create a more just society with a redistribution of wealth unless the levers of economic power were controlled through public ownership.

Labour began as a 'middle-way' party, balanced between trade union working class representatives on the one hand and those from socialist societies on the other. It always accepted from the start that it was a workers' party, seeking working class expression in the House of Commons with men 'sympathetic with the aims and demands of the Labour Movement'. The real cuckoos have been those like Walden who temporarily found themselves in Labour's ranks. Walden says, 'A mighty consensus is developing amongst commentators and academics that socialism no longer has any meaning in the modern Western world'. What he means is that a 'mighty consensus' exists amongst those journalists and commentators who support the present capitalist society and earn a very good living working for it.

I believe revisionism and reformism must be challenged and defeated in the Labour Party. The call for a new socialist party, especially at the present time, is a false one; there are no short cuts to a socialist Britain. We do, however, need to look closely at the Party, and improve the democratic participation of the membership at all levels, especially in the affiliated trade unions. The recent successful ballots for the political levy can be built upon in this connection. It is essential to stop the Party being turned into a glorified electoral machine. Campaigning needs to be closely integrated with the struggles of working people in particular, in factories, offices, shops, the housing estates, in fact wherever workers decide they need to make a stand. It is no good Walworth Road issuing excellent campaign packs about the privatisation of gas, the National Health Service, creating jobs and rebuilding industry, if the miners and Liverpool Labour councillors are publicly repudiated. Such attacks on our own people only help the political enemy and demoralise the troops.

All political parties have to go through periods of change and renewal. If they fail to do so they wither and die and the Labour Party is no exception. If the Party does not renew itself in a socialist direction, if it adopts SDP concepts, it may gain some short term advantages, but in the longer term it will fade into history as it is forced into competition with the Alliance for votes.

At the present time the task for Labour is to win back its lost support and pick up new voters. It will not be able to do this successfully if the people feel they have no real choice. If Labour is to win enthusiastic support it must have a vision of creating a new society, not of patching up what already exists. Over 80 years ago Keir Hardie said, 'If anything is to be really done in this world it must be done by visionaries, by men who see the future, and make the future because they see it'. We need a socialist future, not a half-baked capitalist one. The path the Party takes at the cross roads must be the one leading to socialism.

14
Socialist Internationalism and Labour

The Labour Party has been a member of the Socialist International since 1907. It has a relatively good record on international affairs and was very active in re-forming the International at the end of the Second World War. Although it never, unfortunately, developed an international revolutionary socialist strategy its internationalism, nevertheless, went beyond mere declarations in favour of various movements abroad. Over the years it has given positive support to groups fighting for independence and freedom.

In 1981, the Party produced a discussion pamphlet, *A Socialist Foreign Policy* which outlines the type of policy the Party should be pursuing in foreign affairs. It begins by saying 'In a world threatened by depression and war, internationalism is no longer a dream, but a necessity. We need to co-operate with the international Labour Movement if we are to build a democratic socialist society in Britain. The interaction between our own struggle for socialism and that of others in the world is fully recognised.' It goes on, 'We must challenge the logic that sees no further than armed blocs, counting down to mutual annihilation. Our membership of NATO cannot mean that we allow ourselves to be drawn into the vortex of US foreign policy, particularly as this appears to be returning to the old style imperialist aggression in Central America and elsewhere. To do so would only fuel the new interventionism. While the US is equipping a Rapid Deployment Force to impose its will anywhere in the globe, the Soviet Union has intervened directly in Afghanistan and is actively involved in the Horn of Africa. Such intervention is a violation of the rights of peoples to self-determination. It carries the risk of sparking off regional conflicts which then might escalate to nuclear war engulfing us all'.

The pamphlet emphasises the need for Labour to be on the side of all those fighting injustice: 'The Labour Party is increasingly concerned about the activities of the multi-nationals and their political allies. In so many regimes exploitation goes hand in hand with a denial of democratic and human rights. This is true not only under right-wing dictatorships, but in many countries which proclaim themselves to be socialist. In Eastern Europe dissidents often face repression in the form of labour camps and psychiatric hospitals'. For me, the ideas in this pamphlet form the basis of a clear socialist and internationalist policy.

At the time that *A Socialist Foreign Policy* was published, I chaired the Middle East and Western European Sub-Committees of the Party. I was also an active member of the Latin-American Sub-Committee, often chairing it in the absence of the Chairman. I was, therefore, significantly involved with the drawing up of the pamphlet and later the International Section of the Party Programme. During these years the Party was clarifying its view towards the EEC and, as is well known, it decided to put in the 1983 General Election Manifesto the promise that Labour would take Britain out of the Common Market, after negotiations with the other EEC countries.

The question of the EEC and our attitude to Europe is still with us. The Treaty of Rome has not been substantially altered and if it were to be, it is likely it would be in the direction of a more federal Europe with strengthened powers to the European assembly. How does our call for withdrawal from the Common Market, which has not been overturned by Party Conference, match up with the statement in the pamphlet which says, 'As the world becomes increasingly interdependent the international dimension of Labour's policy becomes increasingly necessary to building a socialist Britain'? Most socialist and communist parties in the EEC see no reason for Britain to leave the Common Market and, because of our position on this matter, question our support for internationalism. When I was Spokes-man on European Affairs in Parliament, and on the Shadow

Cabinet, I had long and sometimes acrimonious discussions with European Socialists, who felt that the Labour Party was letting them down by arguing for withdrawal.

Not all European countries are in the EEC, and some have no wish or intention to join. This is the case with most of the Scandinavian countries as well as Austria and Switzerland. One cannot ignore the EEC, it is a fact of life which affects our legislation and our political and personal lives. I believe we should work for socialist and working-class internationalism in Europe without making the EEC a major issue of contention at the present time, even if some of the European Socialists wish to do so.

I am not saying here that the Party should abandon its position on withdrawal from the EEC, that is still essential. But I do believe that we should step up attempts to bring the left together in all parts of Europe to fight in the EEC, on the Council of Europe, and in all wider European organisations for nuclear disarmament, the phasing out of nuclear power, greater control over the multi-nationals, concerted aid to the Third World, and working class unity in action throughout the European trade union movement.

In 1980, the Labour Party issued another pamphlet, *The Dilemma of Eurocommunism* which, though now bypassed by certain events, does not date in its essentials. Part of its message is that in the EEC it is important that the industrial and political working class movement should, as far as possible, join together in action to fight the multi-nationals, and to put forward an internationalist perspective. Though this will not be easy it must, in my view, be tackled. British socialism cannot build a wall around itself or solve its political and economic problems in isolation. The movement should enter into discussions with all sections of the labour socialist/communist movements in the EEC at the earliest possible moment and at all levels. There are some positive discussions that can take place immediately, not on the basis of defending the Common Market by discussing the best way to operate the capitalist system which exists in the countries of the EEC, but on the basis of what actions we can take in all the EEC countries to spotlight trade union solidarity advocating socialist policies which stretch across national boundaries.

The situation has changed in the Labour Party since I wrote the introduction to *The Dilemma of Eurocommunism*. I said then that '... it may at times be necessary to combat the innate conservatism of the Eurocommunists, who, under certain circumstances, look more gradualist than Britain's Fabian Society'. I think that is still true, but I fear the Labour Party itself is also today showing definite gradualist traits, and there is now little to choose between for example the Communist Party in Italy and the Labour Party in Britain. However, despite their conservatism, both organizations continue to be the parties of and for the working class.

It is important not to confuse the Eurocommunists in Britain with the Communist Party in Italy and other European countries. The British Communist Party is small and unrepresentative, even more so since the split and expulsions. It is looking for allies in all directions. In Italy, the Communist Party is seeking greater political influence, possibly a presence in Government, based on wide support from the mass of the workers. Craxi, the Italian Socialist Leader, had hoped that his Party would attract the workers' vote on as big a scale as the Socialist Party's achievement in France. It has not done so, and in my view will not. More likely is a move by the workers in France back towards the Communist Party, particularly after the disappointing record of the Socialist Party in Government.

I believe the Labour Party should be increasingly internationalist and that is why I feel so strongly about the virtual abolition of the Labour Party's International Department by the Party's present leadership. We cannot, I believe, be taken seriously if it becomes known amongst other Socialist Parties in Europe and elsewhere that Labour no longer has a department concerned solely with international affairs. Personally, I feel very angry about this, especially because it was the British Party which helped re-create the Socialist International and had a number of excellent people whose sole job was dealing with various areas of the world, building up contacts, getting to know the problems and bringing forward to the NEC ideas and proposals for action.

Over the years, NEC members met delegations and individuals from such countries as Nicaragua, Guatemala, Spain and Chile. Such meetings were always useful and important, both to the NEC and to the comrades from those areas. If such meetings are now to be left primarily to the Front Bench, a Parliamentary perspective will be emphasised at the expense of developing solid party links. Not every NEC member is on the Socialist International or the European Confederation of Socialist

Parties, yet it is important that in some way or other they are involved in international contacts and affairs.

The Labour Party, as a Socialist Party, needs to develop its own distinctive foreign policy. We should be arguing that we are neither for Washington nor Moscow but for international democratic socialism. The Labour Party must stand four-square with all those democratic forces who are fighting against US imperialism. That means unqualified support to the Government and people of Nicaragua, and to those fighting for freedom in El Salvador and Guatemala. It must not allow a future Labour Government to even partially backslide as it did over ships and arms for Chile under Pinochet.

Internationalism means real solidarity, even if it costs money. Labour should not be anti-American. Friendship towards the American people is one thing, but snuggling up to American imperialism and supporting US foreign policy is very different. The British labour movement must make it quite clear to Reagan that we will not agree to his policies either on Cruise missiles in Europe or his aggressive stance towards governments in Central and Latin America which do not knuckle under to US policy.

The US Government, through the CIA and multi-national companies, undermined President Allende in Chile and destablised the Chilean economy. It would be foolish on the part of British socialists to believe that the US authorities would not be prepared to do the same here if real socialist policies were being implemented.

The Labour Party's policy on Latin American countries has been a very good one. The one serious blind spot was the Falklands where the discussion document on foreign policy said, 'The Falklands dispute has been deadlocked for years. Party policy is that the inhabitants of the Falkland Islands should not be handed over to a regime which violates human and civil rights. Whilst this remains valid it offers no way out of the stalemate. It is likely that a change of regime in Argentina will be necessary before fruitful tri-partite discussions can be undertaken. Meanwhile, the rights of the Falkland Islanders to self-determination must be upheld'. This led to widespread confusion in the Party when Argentina mounted an invasion.

Policy on Central America is much more clear-cut. The programme states that 'The Labour Party and the Socialist International have come out strongly in support of the anti-imperialist armed struggle currently being waged in El Salvador and Guatemala, in conditions where all peaceful means of opposition are closed, as we did in Nicaragua ... We believe it is essential that Britain under a Labour Government do its utmost to dissociate from American policy in the region and strengthen its independent position'.

The struggle in South Africa is clearly moving towards a climax. Groups in that country who only a few years ago were regarded as moderates are now taking up revolutionary positions. The people of South Africa are on the move and it is they who are setting the political pace. It is vitally important for the Party now to strengthen its links with the African National Congress and South African black trade unionists. This does not mean that Party members should go on jaunts to South Africa. Any visits should be clearly seen as a job on behalf of the movement and should be agreed first with the ANC.

Apartheid is an evil system which, in South Africa, is an essential component in the maintenance of capitalism. Because the two systems are so intertwined, the destruction of apartheid will be a giant step towards the ending of the white South African capitalist system. In *The Political Economy of Race and Class in South Africa*[1] Oliver C. Cox is quoted: 'Our hypothesis is that racial exploitation and race prejudice developed amongst Europeans with the rise of capitalism and that because of the worldwide ramifications of capitalism, all racial antagonisms can be traced back to the policies and attitudes of the leading capitalist people, the white people of Europe and North America'.

In his second court statement from the dock of the Pretoria Supreme Court on 20th April 1964, Nelson Mandela quoted from the Manifesto of Umkhonto, drawn up in 1961, which said 'The time comes in the life of any nation when there remains only two choices — submit or fight. That time has now come in South Africa. We shall not submit and we have no choice but to hit back by all means in our power in defence of our people, our future, and our freedom'. The ANC had hoped to get freedom by peaceful non-violent means, but events forced them to take a more revolutionary position. The Manifesto also states 'We of

---

1. *The Political Economy of Race and Class in South Africa* by Bernard Makhosezwe Magubae. Monthly Review Press.

Umkhonto We Sizwe have always sought to achieve liberation
without bloodshed and avoid clash. We hope, even at this late
hour, that our first actions will awaken everyone to a realisation
of the disastrous situation to which the Nationalist policy is
leading. We hope that we will bring the Government and its
supporters to their senses before it is too late, so that both the
Government and its policies can be changed before matters
reach the desperate stage of civil war'.

The South African Government has, unfortunately, never
come to its senses. Now South Africa stands on the verge of
a bloody civil war which the ANC never wanted. Many brave
black South Africans have already lost their lives. As the battle
intensifies, the Labour Party must make it ever more clear that
it is firmly on the side of the ANC and the oppressed black
masses.

The beginning of Eurocommunism had its roots in the query-
ing of the political system of the Soviet Union by Palmiro Togli-
atti, the Italian communist leader. He developed the concept of
'polycentrism', which stated that the communist world would
have in the future a number of centres — not just one. The
Yugoslav communists had made the initial stand against Stalin,
then the Soviet Chinese disagreement developed, followed by
the Krushev revelations, the Polish Spring, the Hungarian upris-
ing and ultimately the Soviet occupation of Czechoslovakia. It
was quite clear that the situation in the communist world could
never be the same again. Centrifugal forces had always been
present, but now the prestige of the Soviet Union was badly
battered. It was impossible for their leaders to reassert their
total authority, except by force, and that they could only
do when they had military control, as in the Warsaw Pact
countries.

This break down of the authority of the Soviet Union
produced a development which severely tested the commitment
of the Labour Party to those struggling for freedom in Eastern
Europe — the Polish workers formation of Solidarity. It was
clear that the official trade unions in Poland were basically
adjuncts of the State, and instruments of the Party hierarchy.
The workers in Poland wanted a trade union organisation of
their own which was free and independent of the State and the
Party, and which they could control themselves. The fact that
the Church, or at least some of the priests, supported Solidarity
in no way detracts from the importance of the development,

neither does it make the movement of workers basically anti-socialist as some, including left-wing trade union leaders, have suggested.

When I first raised the matter of support for Solidarity on the NEC, I had a tremendous struggle to get my resolution accepted. Some of my natural allies opposed it and one trade union member suggested that Solidarity was not a real union but a breakaway, and therefore it could not be supported. I reminded him that he himself had supported an unofficial movement, in the Seamen's Defence Movement, in his own union years before. That movement had, at one stage, talked of forming a new union and I was one of those who urged them to remain in the NUS and fight to change it because they had the opportunity to do so. In Poland such opportrnities did not exist and the workers had to forge new instruments to make any progress.

The NEC were proved right in giving their support to Solidarity and that was particularly underlined when the miners' strike took place. The Polish Government, like the South African Government, exported coal to this country during the strike. The 'official' unions (Solidarity had been suppressed) did not object and Arthur Scargill and the NUM leaders had to make a strong protest to the head of the Polish Government.

In a foreword I wrote in a pamphlet issued by the Eastern Europe Solidarity Campaign titled *The British Labour Movement and Oppression in Eastern Europe*, I made it clear that in my view it is impossible to create a socialist society without freedom. Socialism and freedom are indivisible. Socialism means the flowering of the human spirit, not its destruction. Yet in parts of the world, oppressive measures have often been taken against critics in the name of socialism. Such actions are a blot on the name of socialism, and have held back the progress of the workers movement in Western Europe for decades. Many trade unionists and workers in the West who over the years have gained hard-won democratic rights and fight to protect them, sometimes unsuccessfully, look at what happens in the so-called 'socialist' countries and say, 'If that is socialism, we want no part of it'.

Within the Labour movement there are, however, a tiny minority who continue to live in the past. They defend just about every action of the Soviet leaders, believing that in doing so they are protecting the Soviet Union from capitalist forces internally and from hostile capitalist elements outside. Because

Soviet diplomats and visitors from the Soviet Union tend to meet predominantly with trade unionists and politicians who hold these views, they get the wrong impression of how their countries' policies are perceived outside. Socialists should at all times attempt to put the record straight.

Dissident groups and individuals seeking democratic changes should receive the support of socialists in the Western capitalist countries, even if we do not always fully or even partly agree with their political ideas or positions. To give such support does not mean that one is siding with those reactionaries who wish to create confrontation and possible war. Unfortunately, the Soviet and other East European communist leaders are helping the reactionary forces by their actions against those who are critical of the regimes. They are, of course, protecting their own privileged positions. If free and open debate took place in these societies, the people would demand changes, just as they did during the Polish Solidarity upsurge, the Hungarian revolution and the Czechoslovakian Spring.

The Italian Communist, the foreign bulletin of the PCI, recently carried details of a symposium in Vienna in September 1985 which included people like Bruno Kreisky, the Austrian ex-Chancellor, Pietro Ingrao of the Italian Communist Party and Peter Glotz, the organisational Secretary of the German Social Democratic Party. The theme of the meeting was, 'Where is Social Democracy Going?' I believe there should be many more such symposiums. It would be a good idea if there could be a Europe-wide one which would include all sections of the working class movement whether they are in the Socialist International or are so-called Eurocommunists. Too often, Western socialists have appeared merely as administrators of the capitalist system rather than as politicians based on the working class, dedicated to ending that system. The movement needs to re-examine what it stands for, and where it is going, and that cannot be left to meetings of leaders of the Parties; it requires much wider participation.

The annual conference in Cavtat, organised by the Yugoslav journal *Socialism in the World* is undoubtedly useful in this regard. It involves Marxists from the East and West, North and South. However, for immediate practical purposes, I believe a conference on an all-European scale is what is required today. At the Cavtat Conference, Pietro Ingrao presented a paper titled 'The European Left and the Problems of a New

Internationalism'. In it he said: 'From its earliest days, the international dimension of the struggle has been a great theme of the workers and socialist movement. We all remember the closing words of the Communist Manifesto. Today, the question of a new internationalism, its content and forms, presses upon us with pregnant urgency'. He goes on to give five reasons for this urgency. They are the acceleration of the arms race, the world crisis and the role of the multi-nationals, the international restructuring of production by multi-nationals involving the powers of national states, the international monetary crisis, and the relations between the Soviet Union and the USA, which in turn concern a whole network of relations between East and West, North and South. Ingrao states that these developments 'Press upon us with fresh immediacy the demand for a new international dimension in our struggle — and I would say in the very organisation of our lives'.

Ingrao is right and that is why we need a socialist internationalist policy. As Ernest Mandel put it in his paper at Cavtat, 'The areas on which self-destruction tendencies are most obvious are the race to acquire nuclear, biological and chemical weapons of mass destruction, and the threats hanging over the ecological balance. This is not the place to enumerate the countless scientific sources which show how current trends may lead to the destruction of human life on earth. In these areas, the alternative is no longer "Socialism or barbarism". It is "Socialism or death".' These are sentiments which I share and are why I believe that socialist internationalism is now more important than ever.

Years ago, Trotsky and others (including the ILP in Britain) raised the necessity of a Socialist United States of Europe. To most people such an idea has always been a pipe dream. Others argue that the EEC actually is the basis of such an organization. My view has changed on this matter. I once believed that the Common Market could have this role and I therefore did not originally oppose our entry. I changed my mind when I realised that under the terms of the Treaty of Rome British workers would suffer for they revealed that the EEC was designed to perpetuate capitalism. Though we should not have any illusions about the EEC leading us into a Socialist Europe, the idea of a workers' Europe based on sound democratic principles is a correct one. Europe is ripe for socialism and if our policies are raised properly as an objective, towards a Europe without nuclear weapons, unemployment and poverty, and for an active positive role in the Third World, they will inspire the young in particular.

There are still many problems in getting the idea of a socialist United States in Europe accepted but the prize is great. Obviously, as things stand at present, there will be many differences of view and approach amongst European Socialists. One major debating point will be around the issue of NATO. My position, which I have made widely known, is that Britain should withdraw from NATO as quickly as possible. To be inside NATO yet against US nuclear weapons and bases seems to me a somewhat contradictory position. In a pamphlet for the Campaign Group, *Peace Through Non-Alignment: The Case Against British Membership of NATO*, Ben Lowe spells out in detail the steps Government must take to eliminate this country's perilous dependence on the USA and its nuclear arsenal. The French are not in NATO, but have their own nuclear weapons. It will be difficult to get them to abandon these arms, but if the whole of the European left urge them to do so, then there should be enough voices in France who will influence the socialists and communists there to fall into line.

Let me conclude by quoting George Lansbury, once leader of the Labour Party whose words on what Labour's foreign policy should be, sum up my own view, 'A Labour Government will not spend many millions a year on armed forces and ... piling armaments. Our foreign policy will not be based on "continuity". Labour will stand for the full and complete right of all nations to rule and administer their own lands'.

15
Socialism and the State

The question of the state and its functions is of immense importance to socialists. There are, as could be expected among socialists a number of differing attitudes to the state and its role. Let me give some contrasting views of different socialists on this issue. Keir Hardie wrote in his book, *From Serfdom to Socialism*[1], 'If it be replied that the state is part of the environment which the owners of property have evolved for their own protection, the obvious answer is that so soon as the working class succeed in capturing and controlling the machinery of State it will then also become part of their natural environment'.

His view was the direct opposite to that of someone like William Paul of the Socialist Labour Party of the early part of the century, who said in his book, *The State — Its Origins and Functions*[2], 'Not only have the Labourists and state "Socialists" been unable to comprehend the nature of the State, they have also failed to understand its social function. Our analysis has shown that the State is the weapon by means of which the ruling-class preserve "order" in a system rent with class struggle and conflicting social interests'.

The matter of whether the existing state could be used, after

---

1. *From Serfdom to Socialism* by Keir Hardie. George Allen, 1907.
2. *The State — Its Origin and Function* by William Paul. Socialist Labour Press 1919.

being captured and controlled by the victorious workers, was discussed at length by Lenin. He categorically stated that the capitalist state machine had to be destroyed and a new one built until the day it withered away.

One can see a very great cleavage in the views of socialists at that time. We now live in a different age and we know that in the Soviet Union, for example, after the Communists took power, the state did not die out but actually became stronger, until to-day when it affects every facet of life. We can see with hindsight that the so-called 'Non-State Socialists' were correct when they argued that state control did not lead to the results desired by the 'State Socialists'. The period of workers' control in industry did not last long in the Soviet Union. It soon gave way to bureaucratic management which was responsible to the state apparatus, which in turn was responsible to the Communist Party, which in its turn was responsible to one person.

The fate of the Soviet revolution is a warning that we have to be clear in our analysis of what the state is. I believe it is important to recognise that the state apparatus has many facets, some of which are the means of class oppression, but others which to some extent serve society as a whole. This is certainly not to say that the class nature of the state has ended, that it is now a neutral force standing above society. The miners' strike should clearly have shattered any illusions on that score. The police, the courts, the law and even the social security system were all used against the miners, just as classical Marxist theory predicted.

William Paul had a point of substance when he wrote, 'Whenever a modern statesman is appointed to control any industrial concern he has to elect expert and permanent officials who know nothing about that industry. These officials are appointed by the State, i.e., from above; they are only answerable to the State Minister who has to depend upon them for all his information regarding his department. The officials are conscious of their power and they use it'. The miners' dispute clearly underlined this analysis. The mining industry, was controlled by a Tory Government, who used the officials of that industry against the miners, at the same time, trying to pretend that they were in no way interfering in the dispute. The state is not above classes in society, and not above class politics.

This is also true in the area of municipal politics. In the past few years Labour Councils have come to the fore with new, local socialist programmes in part copied from the experience of progressive municipalities abroad. According to Raph Samuels in the *New Left Review,* the Greater London Councillors used the book, *Red Bologna*[3] as a sort of bible. Bologna, a Northern Italian City, obtained a left majority (not wholly Communist) in 1975, and a new City administration was set up. It undoubtedly achieved a great deal. It pioneered work in urban planning, in traffic and transport, developed work programmes, had a positive policy on education, a health policy with help to the aged and a social programme. I remember at the time the excitement the book created when it was published, although I felt myself that many Labour councillors in Britain had been doing similar things for some time. Norwich, Sheffield and Manchester were Councils that readily came to mind in this respect.

An important point is made by Sil Schmid in *Red Bologna* that 'However much Bologna's Communist Party (PCI) and Socialist Party (PSI) politicians want to think and act in a socialist manner, they are dependent upon national financial policies ... However progressive the ideas of the Bologna are, in implementing them, they are tied to national law. The Bolognese may be politically conscious and fired by the desire to test new forms of communal life. But subconsciously, in their daily life, they betray the same authoritarian and paternalist attitudes which have stamped their countrymen in Venice and Florence'. The socialists in Bologna suffered from financial and cultural obstacles to their efforts to change society in their area. The second problem could by effort be overcome, but the first was determined by the Government. The State, therefore, would decide.

The same serious problem faces all Labour municipal authorities, who wish to build a sort of non-state municipal society. They are, in the final analysis restricted and controlled by Government legislation and policy. The GLC and the Metropolitan Authorities in their own way decided to try within the overall control of Thatcher capitalism, to create socialist oases in the middle of the capitalist desert. The Government took steps to stop this. Firstly they took London Transport out of the hands of the GLC. Then they decided to abolish all the Metropolitan

---

3. *Red Bologna* — by Max Jaggi, Roger Muller, S. Writers and Readers 1977.

Authorities, including the GLC. They further rolled back the powers of local government by centralising control of the Local Authorities through rate-capping, manipulation of the Rate Support Grant, and various other measures. Municipal social- ism has only a limited role as long as the centralist state is controlled by the Tories.

One of the most thoughtful pieces about the state I have ever read was the article in *New Left Review* 138 by Ralph Milli- band, entitled, 'State Power and Class Interests'. The argument and conclusions of his article are, I believe, fundamentally correct. He explains that the state in the advanced capitalist countries is one of 'partnership between two different, separate forces, linked to each other by many threads, yet each having its own separate spheres of concern'. On the one hand there is the civil aspect of state action with its creation of the Social Security system, the Health Service, the maintenance of roads and so on. On the other there is the repressive side of the state — the judiciary, the police and the military which are used to maintain the power of the predominant class. Milliband points out that the terms of the partnership are by no means fixed, but are affected by circumstance, particularly the condition of the class struggle at a given moment. That is why, for example, under the Thatcher Government, the state is increasingly used as the weapon against the unions and the working class as a whole.

What then is the role of the State under Socialism? Marx, in the *Civil War in France* and Lenin in *The State and Revolution*, claim that state powers would be virtually dissolved with work- ing class power. The state, therefore, 'is not abolished but its functions and powers become largely residual and subordinate'. In a very roundabout way, and in a totally different context, Neil Kinnock expressed a similar view of the future of the state under a future Labour Government when, in his speech at the 1985 Conference (the part of the speech that did not cause any rumpus), he said we had to have 'an enabling state' — a state that would be taken off the people's backs and put under their feet'.

I believe that once Labour has achieved power, with a social- ist programme which it intends to carry out, it will quickly have to turn its mind to the democratisation of those parts of the state apparatus that are used as the instruments of violence, namely the police force and the army. Unless this is done, the ruling class will make use of the fact that the higher echelons of the state are staffed in the main by its own members to mobilise against us. It has happened in other countries and it would be very naive to believe it could not ever happen here.

The police force would, therefore, have to be allowed to have a free trade union that could have some measure of say in the force itself. Furthermore, the police forces would have to come under the direct control of locally elected authorities so that they became the instrument of the people by being fully integrated with them. Similarly, the armed forces would need to be democratised with officers recruited on a wider basis and with the soldiers having the right to belong to a services trade union, affiliated to the TUC. As Ralph Milliband puts it, 'Partnership between state power and class power in a socialist society, means something rather different. It requires the achievement of real power by organs of popular representation in all spheres of life, from the workplace to local government, and it also involves the thorough democratisation of the state system and the strengthening of democratic control upon every aspect of it'.

Milliband rightly argues that state power endures and that it does not 'wither away'. His position is between that of Keir Hardie on the one hand and William Paul on the other. The state will continue, but it will not be the same state under socialism, and its function must be democratically controlled. Even though people like William Paul believed that was impossible, Milliband, I believe, is right.

The State in capitalist society has many different functions. Antonio Gramsci, like all socialist theoreticians concerned with the real world, wrote extensively about it. A large section of his *Prison Notebooks* are taken up with the issue of the state and civil society. He wrote at considerable length about what he called 'Caesarism' and poured scorn on the 'theory of Caesarism', that which claimed that Caesar 'transformed Rome from a City State into the capital of the Empire'. Gramsci wrote, 'Caesarism can be said to express a situation in which the forces in conflict balance each other in a catastrophic manner; that is to say they balance each other in such a way that a continuation of the conflict can only terminate in their reciprocal destruction'. He also talks of 'progressive Caesarism', and 'reactionary Caesarism': 'Caesar and Napoleon I were progressive and Napoleon III and Bismarck were reactionary'. It can be seen that to talk about the state being purely the instrument of a particular class, needs qualification under certain circumstances. The question of the state is not as simple as it seems on the surface.

Gramsci raised the whole question of the Parliamentary system. He wrote in 1933 that, 'It has to be considered whether parliamentarianism and representative systems are synonymous and whether a different solution is not possible — both for parliamentarianism and for the bureaucratic system'. Gramsci's ideas, therefore, have to be seen as a whole. It is no good only looking at one side of his thought; they should all be taken together, and they add up, not to a reformist politician that some would make him but to a revolutionary socialist who believed in a thorough-going transformation of capitalist society.

Gramsci contrasted civil society, which had voluntary autonomous organisations on the one hand, and the state institutions with their coercive character on the other. He believed 'It is possible to imagine the coercive element of the state withering away by degrees, as ever more conspicuous elements of civil society make their appearance'. He recognised that 'Statolatry', what we would call 'Statism', could happen in some backward countries. His attitude was, '... this kind of "Statolatry" must not to be abandoned to itself, must not especially become theoretical functionism or be conceived of as "perpetual".'

I have argued, as Milliband does, that the state will continue after socialists take power. It will have an important role to play, but it must be democratised. That raises the whole question of the state and public ownership. How does public ownership fit in with democratic planning and at the same time develop self-management in industry? There has always been a dichotomy between the two, which, in my view, has never been satisfactorily settled. Nor has it been sufficiently discussed. It is essential to get the correct relationship between the state on the one hand and the workers on the other, otherwise real problems and difficulties, of possibly disastrous proportion, lie ahead.

Without public ownership, the abolition of class power will be impossible. To create socialism, public or social ownership is a necessity. Yet the danger exists, as has been shown in the Soviet Union, that the old class can be replaced by either a new class or a bureaucracy, which is the antithesis of socialism, because an essential cornerstone of socialism is the abolition of class society.

In a series of political essays, *The State and Socialism*[4], Mihaly Vajda, a Hungarian pupil of George Lukacs who was expelled from the Communist Party in Hungary in 1973, wrote, 'I live in a world where the state, which calls itself socialist, is the only real power'. He then quotes Rudolf Bahro, who, he believes, depicts the essential characteristics of 'real existing socialism' in the following way: 'We believed the state would control in favour of society, instead we face a desperate effort to integrate all of living society into the crystallized structure of the state. Statefication instead of socialisation, that means socialisation in a totally alienated form'.

The problem for us as socialists is that some, because they rightly reject the concept of total state control, then throw the baby out with the bathwater, and begin to suggest that private ownership of the means of production is not really a bad thing. The same people claim that because the Soviet Union did not develop into a truly democratic socialist society, the whole theory of Marxism is wrong and that we need a new brand of socialism, a non-Marxist brand. This should worry us less in Britain because British socialists have never accepted the totality of Marxist ideas, and that is not a bad thing. Marx, however, was sufficiently correct in most of his analysis and theory not to be rejected but to be built upon.

Socialism is not indefensible because of the system in Russia for that system is not a truly socialist society. It is a state-controlled economy, but that in itself does not make it socialist. Whilst repudiating the internal lack of democracy in the Soviet Union, and whilst wanting democratic workers' control, we must fully recognise that unless public ownership is carried through, socialism cannot be created. A genuinely just society must be based on an economy that has its factories and work-shops owned in common. Simultaneously, democratic forms of workers' management must be developed. The only real way to socialism is for common ownership and democratic management to come together. There must also be an input through consumer organisations.

It is also essential under socialism for the political system to be pluralist. Politicians must compete with each other through parties and groups for the vote and support of the people, a

---

4. *The State and Socialism* by Mihaly Vajda. Allison & Busby 1981.

view very clearly expressed by Rosa Luxemburg. It is possible that the Parliamentary system in time could, as Gramsci suggests, give way to some other form of representation. But whatever the form, democracy itself, in the widest possible sense, is essential.

I fully appreciate why those who have suffered imprisonment in the East, or have been weighed down by the nature of the bureaucratic system there, have become hostile to the very idea of socialism. Yet when some do come to the West, and live under capitalist conditions, they are not particularly enamoured with the system here either. Not all of those who have left the Soviet Union and the other East European countries have become anti-socialist. Some want to see democracy created in their own countries together with a new political system, not the return of capitalism as we know it in the West.

The state, therefore, must not become all powerful. If it were to wither away altogether that would be a positive development, but it is a long time off. In the meantime, a democratised state must be used to carry out policies beneficial to the people — maintaining a National Health Service; preventing people from living in poverty; running national systems for electricity, gas, oil and other energy, and so on. We have to get the balance right, and learn from past mistakes, both in Britain and especially in the so-called 'existing socialist states'.

In Britain we live in an old capitalist country and are encumbered by many antique institutions which serve to perpetuate the domination of a secret, privileged and hide-bound ruling class. The workings of the Civil Service, the judiciary and, indeed, the Palace of Westminster itself with its hereditary element, are geared to the reproduction of inequality and the exclusion of ordinary people from real participation in shaping the direction of society. This is not the place to explore in detail all the reforms democratic socialists must insist upon but the Campaign Group has proposed a far-reaching series of urgent democratic measures including abolition of the House of Commons, transfer of the royal perogative to the Speaker, a Freedom of Information Act, trade union rights for the armed services, wide-ranging enabling powers for municipal and regional government, a Bill of Rights to protect and extend civil liberties and to bring under control all the agencies of the state. It is my conviction that the elitist and oligarchic state we have in Britain has to be challenged by any democratic socialist worthy of the name and that only a concerted barrage of reforms will do the job.

Socialists need not be divided into state socialists and non-state socialists any more than they need to be divided into revolutionaries and reformists. It is merely important that those who genuinely believe in socialism should learn from each other. There have been state socialists who considered themselves revolutionaries, like the Bolsheviks, and others, the Fabians for example, who were reformists. The same can be said for non-state socialists. The old SLP were revolutionaries, G.D.H. Cole was a reformist. All were right and wrong on some points. They were, however, agreed on essentials, that the world could only become a better place if socialism was created.

If the State can help advance a socialist society, then it should be used. If it does not, and it becomes all-powerful, then it should be changed and, if necessary, destroyed. The state, however, must play a secondary role. The socialism of the future, that which can create a more human society that can genuinely liberate man and womankind, is self-management based on the various forms of common ownership. With self-management of industry and genuine pluralist democracy in politics, the fear of a new class or vast bureaucratic structure can be eliminated.

16
Democratic Socialism and Revolutionary Reformism

The concept of socialism was first mooted in a practical sense during the English Revolution which established the rising capitalist class as the dominant class in English society. It made Parliament politically supreme and even the Monarchy, when restored in 1660, was dependent upon Parliament for its future. The British ruling-classes are quite happy to keep the Monarch, but soon make it clear who really holds the power if they feel the occasion warrants it.

The ideas of socialism have been around since the period of the primitive Christian Church. In England, a type of communism was taught and argued for during the Peasants' Revolt of 1381. It was St. Isodore who defined natural law in the following terms. 'They preach Plato and prove it by Seneca, that all things under Heaven ought to be in common'. John Wycliffe, the theologian, who argued strongly for a type of communism saying 'the possessions of the unrighteous were acquired by rapine, theft, robbery and usurpation', pointed out that in ACTS IV 32 'the Apostles held everything in common'.

Another important fighter for communistic ideas was the 'Hedge Priest', John Ball. It was Ball who, looking back to the origins of society asked the question 'When Adam delved and Eve span — Who was then the Gentleman?' According to Froissard in his *Collection de Chroniques*[1], Ball once said, 'My

1. *Collection de Chroniques* by Froissard from *A History of British Socialism* by M. Beer. Allen and Unwin, 1953.

good people — Things cannot go well in England, nor ever will, until all goods are held in common, and until there will be neither serfs nor gentlemen, and we shall be equal. For what reason have they, whom we call Lords, got the best of us? How did they deserve it? Why do they keep us in bondage? If we all descended from our father and our mother, Adam and Eve, how can they assert or prove that they are more masters than ourselves? Except perhaps that they make us work and produce for them to spend'. Ball gave his full support to the Peasants' Revolt, and after their defeat he met a violent end on the gallows at St. Albans in my native country, Hertfordshire.

The pre-cursors of modern socialism were undoubtedly the Diggers or true Levellers during the Civil War, their spokesmen being Gerrard Winstanley and William Everhard who had been in the Cromwellian Army. Winstanley, who has been described as the fiery soul of the Digger movement, was in fact a sort of peaceful John Ball. He was a medieval communist in theory who rejected any idea of using violence. He it was who argued that all land should be owned in common, saying, 'There shall be no buying and selling of earth, nor the fruits thereof'.

In his *Law and Freedom*[2], he wrote, 'The earth is to be planted and the fruits reaped and carried into barn and store-house by the assistance of every family with corn or other provisions, they may go to the storehouse and fetch without money. If they want a horse to ride, they may go into the fields in summer or to the common stables in winter, and receive one from the keepers and when the journey is performed bring him back. All the labour of husbandmen and tradesmen within the country shall be upon the common stock. And as everyone works to advance the common stock so every one shall have free use of any commodity in the storehouse for his pleasure and comfortable livelihood, without buying or selling or restraint from anybody'.

The 1830s saw the appearance of the Chartists, the first workers' movement in the world, which put forward a number of demands for 'Universal suffrage, vote by ballot, annual Parliaments, no property qualifications, payment of MPs, equal electoral districts, the separation of Church and State, the restoration of that portion of Church property taken from the poor

---

2. *Law of Freedom* by Gerrard Winstanley, 1652.

back to its rightful owners, a voluntary system of education, the abolition of capital punishment, the abolition of the new Poor Law, a system of direct taxation ...'

Democracy is therefore deeply rooted in the British working-class movement. The Labour Party today is part of that democratic tradition and one can only hope that it never discards such a magnificent heritage. Democracy is something the working class movement has fought for over a long period, often by hard and bitter struggle. Socialism and democracy are synonomous. In a way there is no such thing as 'democratic socialism' but only socialism. If it is not democratic, it is not real socialism.

Democratic socialists believe in a free press. We reject the idea of a state press, putting forward only the views of the Government or the ruling party. I am not one who argues that today we do not have some freedom of the press. But the British press is manipulated, and often — especially this is true of some of the 'popular' papers — deformed in the interests of maintaining the capitalist free enterprise system. Arguments within the Labour Party, for example, are personalised by headlines like 'Benn gives his Orders', or 'Benn's policy to abolish the House of Lords', 'Callaghan Hits Back' and so on. We see the sinister cartoons which show, for example, Tony Benn and myself with hammers and sickles, or standing with KGB men, alongside snide comments, insinuating that we are against Parliamentary democracy and for dictatorship. Some of this dangerous material unfortunately influences people because, from time to time, I receive letters from those who have obviously been deceived by what they have read in the newspapers.

Nye Bevan, particularly suffered from the attentions of the newspapers and is reported as once saying that Britain had the most prostituted press in the world. In the second volume of his book on Bevan, Michael Foot writes '... Some ill-wishers saw these operations in a sinister light: "Bevan crisis weekend. He has two plans to grab the socialist leadership" ran the headlines in the *Sunday Express* of 3rd February; a tale followed of how the plotters had been assembling at 23, Cliveden Place. It was all a fabrication and Bevan took the rare step of issuing a public denial ... No word of apology or of withdrawal appeared in the *Daily Express* or *Sunday Express*, and a little while later, Arthur Deakin returned to the subject in a speech at Bristol'. Then, as now, even Labour and trade union leaders are sometimes misled by what they read in the papers.

The press has not always been the defender of the establishment. When papers were first published in Britain, most of them were democratic in orientation, and there was a great struggle to get them circulated without high taxes which put them out of reach of the working man and woman. A group of radical democrats set out to get rid of the Newspaper Stamp Act, and in a report they said they objected 'to the limitation imposed by the Stamp upon the circulation of the best newspapers, and to the impediment which it throws in the way of the diffusion of useful knowledge regarding current and recent events among the poorer class, which species of knowledge relating to subjects which most obviously interest them, call out the intelligence by awakening the curiosity of these classes — apart from financial consideration, they do not consider that news itself a desirable subject for taxation'.

The struggle for press freedom is only a part of socialists' broader fight to extend the frontiers of democracy and extend genuine freedom to society as a whole, the very opposite of the charges made by our denigrators. As R.H. Tawney put it, 'The British version of socialism, therefore, has democracy as its basis. In labouring to add new economic storeys to the house, it has no intention of destroying its political foundations. Its attitude to freedom is no exception to that statement. It involves, not the curtailment of liberties, but their more general extension, and is for that reason denounced as tyrannical by those whose authority is likely, as a consequence, to suffer diminution. Classes at the top may fall, but cannot rise. The construction which they put on freedom is the result of that position'.

As socialists, we should expect the establishment to fight us. It has never been known to surrender power and privilege easily. They fight strongly to preserve what they have. It is for this reason that they are so incensed about Labour's proposal to abolish the House of Lords. The Lords is a bastion of privileges of the British ruling class. Their powers are used ruthlessly against Labour Governments, but are equally useful when they believe their own Tory Government might be making a political mistake, which could cost it votes in the country.

The Labour Party, at its Annual Conference as far back as 1932, passed a resolution calling for the abolition of the Lords. A resolution similar in many respects was passed in 1978. The reaction of Conservative politicians in 1932 was almost exactly the same as to-day. One ex-Minister at the time demanded that there should be a revision in the powers of the House of Lords so that in future a Labour House of Commons would be unable to carry out its socialist policy. An ex-Deputy Speaker insisted that, unless that was done it might be necessary to revise the Royal Veto against legislation hostile to what he described as 'economic privilege'.

Tory Conferences have revealed that there are Tory plans to reform the House of Lords in order to strengthen its powers, with some genuflection towards democratic concepts failing to disguise its clear intended role as a body designed to make socialist policies even more difficult to carry through. The Lords is an out-dated, undemocratic chamber and only comes to life occasionally, either to preserve the status quo or defend the interests of the Tory Party. The time for non-elected people to have a say in our legislation and a seat in Parliament purely because of parentage or a Prime Minister's patronage has long passed.

There are those who argue, even in the Labour Party, that the House of Lords should be replaced by a Second Chamber, appointed, semi-elected or fully elected. That is not the view of the Party itself — Labour's 1978 Conference called for total abolition of the House of Lords. It recommended a one-chamber democratic House of Commons with built-in safeguards so that a Government could not be self-perpetuating against the people's will. Such a uni-cameral system exists in the democracies of New Zealand and Sweden and both are strong democratic countries. There is no reason why things should be different here.

In Chile, before Pinochet, there were two chambers, and the second chamber of Senators which was electorally weighed to assist the election of right-wing candidates was used to stop President Allende from carrying out his policies. The Senators, through their obstructive tactics, were responsible for much of the decline in the economic situation in Chile.

If second chambers have proved so obstructive to progressive policies then why do democratic socialists believe that socialism in Britain can be achieved through Parliament? It is a question which those on the left, who are democratic socialists, but who believe in revolutionary socialist policies, cannot avoid facing up to. There have been plenty of examples where democratically elected, progressive socialist Governments have been overthrown by force. Hitler destroyed democracy in Germany,

Mussolini in Italy, Franco in Spain, the colonels in Greece, the military in Turkey. Unfortunately, in most countries in the world, democracy is weak and dictatorship is strong. Democracy under certain circumstances could be destroyed here but Labour will never do anything to endanger it. We are opposed to the use of force to remove opposing political forces and the only occasions on which Labour might resort to it would be in the defence of democracy, as the Austrian socialists did when they fought to try to preserve democracy in their country in 1934. The Labour Party is not a pacifist party and there are occasions when anti-democratic forces have to be dealt with in a democratic society. But it is essential to make sure that in the process all the basic democratic rights of the people are protected.

Parliament must be used by Labour as the means to transform society. The first few months of a Labour Government will be decisive for it is then that much essential legislation can be enacted. If Labour is obstructed in this by an undemocratic House of Lords, the issues should be put to the people. The machinery of Government, especially of the Civil Service, will have to be reformed and there will have to be a radical reduction of patronage at all levels.

But democracy should not stop at the door of government. A truly democratic socialist party must also fight for the extension of democratic processes at the place of work. One of the most serious criticisms of past nationalisation is that it has been bureaucratic. The cry has rightly been that the workforce itself has not been sufficiently involved. Apart from isolated cases, industrial democracy has never really existed in the publicly-owned industries.

When the steel industry was nationalised, a number of worker-directors were placed on the main Board. It soon became clear that the creation of these posts was only a gesture towards democratic management. It is not a token group of worker-directors which is required but methods of democratic control which allow self-management by the entire workforce. This is not a pipe dream. It is interesting to note that every time an upsurge takes place in the Eastern European Communist countries, the demand by the workers is for workers' control of industry. They do not want to return to capitalism, they want to keep their public industries, but they also want a real say in how their industries are run and organised. This same demand has arisen in Britain at different times.

There is some confusion about industrial democracy. It is really an umbrella term which means different things to different people. It can sometimes mean good industrial relations with proper bargaining between the employers and workers. It can mean workers exercising control over their employers, or even a Government, but not actually managing industry. It can also mean the democratic management of industry by the workers through elected workers' councils. Democratic management is what socialists should be aiming for, and what the Labour Party would eventually like to see introduced. Our concept of democratic management is, however, very different from the German works Councils which have no real say in how their companies are run. The TUC is opposed to such Councils being introduced in Britain, but is divided as to whether unions should become involved in management.

The answer is for the unions to retain their role as bargainers whilst the workers in the industry seek self-management. To avoid syndicalism — ownership purely by the workers acting independently in each plant, or within an industry — it will be necessary to integrate workplaces and sectors into a National Plan, with the Government having a real involvement to ensure that the industry concerns itself with national consumer interests.

Many ideas have been advanced over the years as to how the workers in Britain could run their industries. The greatest exponent of democratic management was Professor G.D.H. Cole who outlined his ideas in a series of books and pamphlets. His *Self-Management in Industry*[3] is a socialist classic. His ideas were taken up in Yugoslavia, after that country broke with the Soviet Union and its Stalinist concepts. The Labour Party should begin by introducing Professor Cole's ideas into the main nationalised industries. It should not, however, be tied to any particular scheme of democratic management. It should be flexible and allow the workforce to develop its own ideas as to how to democratically manage a plant, company or industry.

It would be absurd to believe that every worker could become a technically advanced manager but all can participate

---

3. *Self-Management in Industry* by G.D.H. Cole.

in the formulation of decisions for their plant and industry. Modern management is advanced in its techniques but it is clear that workers can often be very sophisticated in their ideas too. Many shop steward committees have produced their own plans, dealing with complex and difficult matters, to save a company or industry from closure or to switch to socially useful production.

The Labour Party bases its policies for industrial democracy on Clause IV of the Party Constitution. It also takes into consideration the bitter experiences that workers have had over the past years, when company after company has closed down with the workers receiving minimum prior information, still less consultation. Workers should be fully informed about what is happening in their industries. Both private and public corporations should give the general public the fullest information. The Labour Party wants to see the fullest involvement of the people at all levels of the democratic process. They should be given the facts and allowed to decide without manipulation by financial or other interests.

As socialists are for democracy in the workshop they are also against all forms of racialism. Racialism is a destructive force which turns people against people, nation against nation, and creates irrational hatreds which can lead to mass destruction. We have only to remember what happened in Germany under Hitler. The Nazis used the Jews as a scapegoat for the country's economic failure and millions died in concentration camps. Lies were spread about Jews, as lies are being spread in Britain today about ethnic minority groups.

Racialism is not only anti-socialist, it is also anti-Christian. Jesus is often shown surrounded by children of all races and colours under the words, 'Suffer little children to come unto me'. He did not say suffer little white children, or black children, but just children. The message is clear. We are all God's children, irrespective of race, creed or colour.

It is easy to set white worker against black worker and to play upon prejudices which can easily be blown up because of cultural differences and historical backgrounds. The Labour Party has set its face against such racial prejudice. It believes that where there are problems these have to be dealt with in a serious, yet generous and courageous way. All forms of discrimination have to be fought. All citizens, irrespective of colour or national background, must be treated equally.

At the moment, there is widespread unemployment. It affects white, black and brown workers. It is not caused by there being too many coloured workers in Britain, but an economic system in which unemployment is endemic. The problems of unemployment can only be overcome when we organise our resources, plan our production, create and develop new industries, and get sensible agreements with other countries on trade and financial matters.

Britain to-day is a multi-racial society. That does not mean that we all have to be the same, or even love each other. But it does mean that we have to live together in mutual respect, recognising and protecting each other's rights and learning from each other. Although there are serious problems, I personally believe the British people are sufficiently tolerant to overcome them. I believe we can create a racially harmonious society in which, in the long run, we can all live together without even noticing that people are of a different colour or from a different racial background. Only societies where racism has been extinguished can be considered truly democratic.

If tackling racism in our society is a priority for Labour, so too is the confronting of sexism and the oppression of women. Women have particular problems, and particular needs. In the past, socialists have tended to believe that women's liberation will automatically be settled once a socialist society is created. That to a large extent was the view of Alexander Kollontai. She said in a speech entitled 'The Women Workers in Contemporary Society', 'There is no independent women's question, the woman question arose as an integrated part of the social problems of our time. The liberation of woman as a member of society, a worker, an individual, a wife, and a mother, is possible therefore only together with the solution of the general social question, with the fundamental transformation of the present social order'.

Kollontai was correct, up to a point, but she implies that the struggle for women's rights and equality has to wait until the establishment of socialism. That is not a view the women of today would accept and they are right not to do so. Even now, before socialism is created, equality can be fought for in the labour movement, and especially in the Labour Party. Women, for example, should have directly elected representatives on the NEC chosen either at their own Women's Conference or by women delegates at the Party Conference.

The struggle for socialism is part of the struggle for women's equality. It is also the struggle for the rights of homosexuals and lesbians. All these groups suffer in class dominated society. The Labour Party, therefore, in developing social policies and fighting for socialist ideas, must act as the unifying force which will bring all these groups together.

Another important part of the fight against the continuation of the capitalist system is the fight for conservation. We have seen in West Germany, over the past decade in particular, the growth of the so-called 'Greens'. They have undoubtedly changed the political map in West Germany and have had a real impact on the base of the SPD. The Labour Party must become the 'Green Party' in Britain if it is to avoid a similar fate.

In an interesting and important article in *New Left Review* 152, 'Eco-Politics in West Germany', Werner Halsberg points out that the 1983 Programme of the Greens favoured the introduction of the 35 hour week as something that should be achieved as soon as possible. The document said, 'The struggle in the factories and trade unions is essential above all for the achievement of shorter working time, more humane working conditions and changes in the wage structure. Strikes and factory occupations should be increased to save jobs and prevent closures. But one of the goals of such struggles must be the transformation of plant towards socially and ecologically useful production and self-management'.

Halsberg points out that the majority of the Greens in West Germany have supported the fight for the 35 hour week, that they supported the miners' strike in Britain, and that some have called for the nationalisation of the steel industry in Germany as the solution to the steel crisis.

At the moment, the Ecological Party in Britain is not strong, but its potential is there and if the Labour Party turns away from its role in transforming and humanising society, it will be they, rather than Labour, who will find increased support. One central feature of the Green's policy has been the issue of environmental protection. That is surely something which will increasingly loom large in Britain. We already have the debate about the future of nuclear power, with many up in arms about the nuclear waste which is polluting the Irish Sea and the British coastline. Recently, tests have shown that the levels of mercury in the Mersey estuary are so high that fish in the river are being affected by it. At the same time, acid rain is destroying trees and plants and children are being poisoned by lead in petrol exhaust from cars. The Socialist Environment and Resources Association (SERA) was set up to tackle problems like these. Its general aims are: 1) To ensure that the present and future generations live in a healthy and stable environment. 2) To identify the social, economic and political causes of environmental problems and formulate socialist policies, to deal with them. 3) To develop practical alternative projects or programmes to those SERA object to on social and environmental grounds. 4) To promote these policies and programmes in the labour movement, and 5) To promote the election of socialist candidates who are in broad sympathy with SERA's aims.

In a SERA pamphlet, *Socialism and Ecology*, Professor Raymond Williams, a Vice President of SERA, argued against those who claim that conservationists are seeking salvation in some pre-industrial haven, a similar charge which was made in the past against William Morris. Williams writes, 'It is not really a matter of choice whether we can go on with certain existing patterns and conditions of the resources of the earth with all their damage to life and health. The central issues of world history over the next 20 or 30 years are going to be the distribution and use of these resources'. He goes on to argue that war over resources is a real danger, and that 'we can properly link the argument about resources, about their equal distribution and renewal, with the argument about the avoidance of war'.

SERA puts forward a non-state socialist position, something strongly argued for in a booklet by Alan Taylor, *Democratic Planning through Workers' Control*. He explains that neither unemployment, pollution nor resource wastage can be solved by central planning, state ownership, worker participation or collective bargaining, as 'none make the use of capital directly answerable to either workers or the community'. The answer for Taylor lies only in workers control.

According to SERA, the central failing of the Labour Party's policy is its continuing belief in economic growth and the extension of central planning. I believe there is some merit in their argument but, as I have argued elsewhere, it is important for both the state to have a role and for there to be democratic control over the state. SERA themselves believe that public intervention, as a means of ensuring environmental improvements, is necessary and they would like to see it extended to agriculture with a stricter pollution control.

They argue that Labour's 1983 Manifesto, 'The New Hope for Britain' is inadequate on environmental issues and that the Party has some way to go before it can really claim to be the 'British Green Party'. I must say, despite the new and better document recently issued on the environment by the NEC, I agree with them.

I have argued in this book that the Labour Party is at the crossroads. It has made important socialist gains in policy and organisation over the years, but those gains are now being pushed back. The difficulty which left-wing socialists face in the Party today is that they, more than anyone else, want the defeat of the Thatcher Government, and because of that are reluctant to raise legitimate criticisms of the way in which the Party is going. I believe the best way to win the election is to be bold, to argue the socialist case unflinchingly and not to pretend that we do not want to change society in any fundamental way. It is important to remember that the Tories under Mrs Thatcher came out boldly for their type of reactionary Toryism and won. People like to know what political parties stand for and what they intend to do.

The Labour Party needs to be a socialist campaigning party, not merely a party dominated by its media image. Unfortunately that is the direction in which we seem to be going at present. The Party today continues to issue a multiplicity of campaign documents and charters on different subjects. They contain many good proposals which rightly should be campaigned for. The document at the centre of Labour's industrial policy is *A New Partnership* drawn up by the Labour Party/TUC Liaison Committee. It was discussed and accepted at both the TUC and Labour Party Conferences, and contained a lot of good material. Its basic weakness is that it fails miserably to put forward a socialist perspective. It retreats from the policies that have been put forward by the Party in the past. Both Tony Benn and I tried to get it strengthened in a socialist direction at the Liaison Committee and the NEC, but failed to get sufficient support.

Now, at the time of writing, the Party is working on a Charter for Industrial Democracy. It proposes firstly that industrial democracy is the key to a stronger economy, secondly, that Tory confrontation with the unions does not solve problems but

makes them worse, and thirdly, that Labour's aim is a new partnership with rights for workers. I find this new partnership
concept to be a strange notion for the Labour Party and trade
union movement to put forward. The only partnership there has
ever been in industry, under private capitalism, is the very
junior 'partnership' of workers to those who own the industry,
make profits from it and use them to perpetuate the class system
of society. Sometimes the interests of workers and employer run
parallel in a particular industry, and when they do, a temporary
arrangement to co-operate can be made, but it is hardly a partnership. Even when workers are involved in management
decisions about the future of a company or industry they
cannot, in the long term, make much difference to the way it is
run if profits remain the key objective.

The central questions for socialists are who owns an industry,
and what can be done to control the future of that industry
through democratic socialist planning? By talking about a new
partnership the Labour Party and TUC are indulging in make-
believe. That is especially true now that most of the publicly-
owned industries have been privatised and are working under
private enterprise profit-making criteria.

Many of the proposals in the Charter for Industrial Democracy are important ones. The Party is pledged to repeal the
Tory anti-union laws and replace them with new legislation.
There is also talk of a new Bill of Rights though we must be
careful that this is not another 'In Place of Strife' under a new
name. (The new policy document 'People at Work: New Rights,
New Responsibilities' has now been agreed by the NEC and the
General Council of the TUC. However a minority on both
bodies oppose the document in certain aspects concerning
future statutory legislation affecting the internal affairs of trade
unions.) The Charter also suggests that there will be new rights
to information, consultation and representation through joint
union committees. There will also be 'Euro-initiatives' tied to
the directives of the EEC. Obviously it is important to see
exactly what is involved in these measures but the directives in
themselves are miles away from the real industrial democracy
proposed in the past by G.D.H. Cole. It is to Cole's proposals
that we should be looking if we are not to be tied down to tired
old policies, which have no real appeal to the majority of
workers in industry.
information, consultation and representation through joint

union committees. There will also be 'Euro-initiatives' tied to the Vredeling and directives of the EEC. Obviously it is important to see exactly what is involved in these measures but the directives in themselves are miles away from the real industrial democracy proposed in the past by G.D.H. Cole. Yet it is to Cole's proposals that we should be looking if we are not to be tied down to tired old policies, which have no real appeal to the majority of workers in industry.

The type of policy required is what I have described for want of a better phrase, 'Revolutionary Reformism.' To some extent Cole was the precursor of that concept, although he never used the phrase. In 1954, he wrote a pamphlet published by the *New Statesman and Nation*[4] in which he said 'This pamphlet is about Socialism, by which I mean a society without class, and not one in which a new class structure has replaced the old. It is not about the policy to be followed by a Labour Government which is not seeking to establish a classless society, but only to nationalise a few more industries and add a few more pieces to the equipment of the Welfare State. It is an attempt to indicate a way of action for those socialists who feel a sense of frustration because to them Socialism means something radically different from the management Welfare State ... If we mean to constitute a really democratic society, permeated by the spirit of social equality, we shall have to find ways of replacing old incentives of fear and habit with new inducements more consistent with the recognition of equal human rights ... Social ownership is only half the battle; the other half is real participation by the workers in control — not only at the top, but at every level from the work group upwards. By participation I do not mean merely consultation; I mean real control'.

At the moment, despite the new NEC document on social ownership, we are neither being offered real social ownership nor real control by the workers. With the concept of 'new partnership' we are back in the realms of Gaitskell's pamphlet, *Industry and Nationalisation*, Tony Crosland's *The Future of Socialism*, John Strachey's *Contemporary Capitalism* and the Party Policy Statement of 1957, *Industry and Society*.

No doubt the type of policies I put forward will be classified

---

4. *Is This Socialism?* by G.D.H. Cole. New Statesman and Nation in association with the Fabian Society, 1954.

by old friends in the SWP as 'left reformist' which, they say, is the counter to 'right reformism' in the Labour Party. It is a charge I will have to live with. Stafford Cripps, in 1932, wrote a pamphlet, *Can Socialism Come by Constitutional Means?* His answer to this question was 'Yes, but only just', and I agree with this position. He also said, absolutely correctly, that 'We must face the fact that those who at present hold the economic power will refuse their support to any Labour Government. The idea that if the Labour Party is gentle and well-behaved it will persuade the capitalists to hand over the economic power to the Government is quite fantastic'.

I believe that *Socialist Worker*, which the SWP produce, is a good socialist newspaper. But I think the SWP are wrong to be outside the Labour Party, with their separate revolutionary organization. They are also wrong when they argue that there is no chance of socialism being created through the Parliamentary road. They say, for example, in the introduction to their pamphlet, *The Labour Party — Myth and Reality* by Duncan Hallas, that the miners split the Labour Party wide open. That is not true — the Party was solidly behind the miners and it was only some of the PLP leaders who were not wholeheartedly for the strike. Though the leader claimed to be impartial in condemning the violence of the police and the violence of the pickets, that was not the position of the overwhelming majority of the Party membership. Duncan Hallas has obviously not read the NEC resolution on the matter, nor taken note of the demonstration in the House of Commons, led by myself, when forty Labour MPs stood in front of the Mace and the House was suspended.

The SWP are guilty of simplification when they suggest that no Labour Government has advanced socialism in any way. Such Governments could have done more, it is true, but they certainly defended workers rights to a greater extent than Tory governments have. The SWP are wrong, in my view, to say socialists should now leave the Labour Party and join with them in building a new organization. They have issued a call to Militant supporters to join them outside the Labour Party glossing over the basic theoretical difference between them which centres on the attitude they adopt towards the nature of the Soviet Union. Perhaps the SWP are now taking my view which is that I do not know whether the Soviet Union is state capitalist or a deformed workers' state with a bureaucracy but I do know that it is not socialist.

Talk of leaving the Party ignores the fact that nothing remains static and the Party will not either. There may be a temporary resurgence of right-wing strength, due to the present position of the leadership, but that cannot and will not last forever. Though it would be counter-productive to challenge the leadership prior to the next General Election it is possible, and indeed necessary, for the left to agree on a number of issues on which to fight and to go out in the party and win support for them.

What, then, is our future perspective? Labour will go into the next election with the present leadership and policies determined by it, policies which by the time the election comes will undoubtedly be very different from those we advanced at the last General Election. At the time of writing the leadership is holding firm on its policy on nuclear weapons, and it maintains that it does not agree to a coalition with the SDP. On other issues, however, the watering down process is well under way and wholesale, but surreptitious, revisionism is taking place. We could therefore find ourselves with a Labour Government, which on some issues such as public ownership, is very much worse than previous Labour Governments. Even some of our policies on the Welfare State look as if they will be diluted. Socialism is hardly mentioned by the current leadership and a socialist society is not the objective being advanced. What then should be the strategy of those who do believe in creating a socialist society with a Labour Government as the instrument of change? Firstly, it must not be on the basis of keeping quiet and saying and doing nothing until the Labour Government is elected. That would be wrong. But, secondly, neither can it think in serious terms of challenging the present leadership. It must be on the basis of demanding (a) that present policy be adhered to, such as non-nuclear policy, and (b) that we put before the people a truly socialist perspective.

We must not, in the face of this revisionism, keep our heads down until Labour is elected. We must openly argue for the public ownership of the banks and the land; the abolition of the House of Lords and all the privileges that go with it; the re-nationalisation of those publicly-owned industries which have been privatised without massive compensation and possibly in some cases without any compensation at all; the reduction of hours without loss of pay to even lower than a 35 hour week; the repeal of all anti-trade union legislation and restoration of legislation giving workers rights they previously enjoyed; and a system of genuine workers' management in industry, along the lines outlined by G.D.H. Cole and others.

We should also campaign for the right to a free press, the first step to this being legislation for the right of reply; full freedom of information to the workers in industry, but also to all citizens through a Freedom of Information Act which would take the mystery out of Government; the democratization of the Civil Service, and the police; and a socialist foreign policy that is distinctive and neutralist, which clearly shows that we do not accept the hegemony of either Moscow or Washington.

These are the policies which the left must continue to advocate, with maximum vigour, in the run up to the next election. In addition we should be arguing inside the Party for a number of organisational strategies. Firstly, we should call on the Party to build branches in every factory, workshop, mine, construction site and office. Factory branches were agreed by the Party a few years ago, but have not yet been vigorously pursued. Secondly, the Party must seriously consider the democratic involvement of all the membership in both elections and the development of policy. At the moment participation in policy-making is very patchy and could be greatly improved. Thirdly, we must emphasise the importance of involving Black and Asian people in the work of the Party. That means appointing full-time organisers in this area and going beyond the present policy of setting up Ethnic Minority Committees. I believe the Black and Asian comrades must have direct representation on the NEC. Fourthly, the Party must build a mass membership, with the objective of having party groups within the branches in every street and block of flats in the country.

Fifthly and finally, we should point out that the time has come to create a really effective political education programme. This should not be solely concerned with organising work for elections, but with teaching the political theory of socialism and developing the organisation to put that theory into effect. Since the demise of the NCLC there has not been an effective socialist educational organisation, and the Party should move quickly to create one. The recent appointment of a national Political Education Officer is an important step in this direction. Such an organisation could hold classes during the day for the unemployed and other classes in the evening for workers. It could organise postal courses, conferences, and week schools with a particular emphasis on socialist economics, philosophy, history, literature, and organisation.

The present emphasis on organisation and image-building is misplaced. Important as organisation is, unless the membership is enthused to support Party policy, it will make no real progress. Policy and organisation must go hand in hand. The membership must be convinced that it is a better world we are seeking, not simply getting politicians into Parliament for their own personal aggrandisement.

This then is the real choice: Are we to go forward to rebuild and develop the Party as an instrument of socialism, that will fight for a socialist Britain as part of a socialist world, or are we to be a party which waters down its socialism, and settles for managing capitalism. The argument as to what the future holds will continue for a number of years. It will not be settled between now and the next General Election. That is why we have to concentrate on winning that election, whatever our views and despite our fears. Neither the Tory Government nor the SDP/Liberal Alliance offer any hope to the British people for the future. Only socialism, achieved through the election of a radical Labour government, can do that. Our objective was well put by Keir Hardie in *From Serfdom to Socialism*[5] when he wrote: Socialism implies the inherent equality of all human beings. It does not assume that all are alike, but only that all are equal ... (it) implies brotherhood, and brotherhood implies a living recognition of the fact that the duty of the strong is not to hold the weak in subjection, but to assist them to rise higher and ever higher on the scale of humanity, and that this cannot be done by trampling upon and exploiting their weakness but by caring for them and showing them the better way'.

---

5. *From Serfdom to Socialism* by Keir Hardie. George Allen (London), 1907.